Toward a New Iron Age?

Toward a New Iron Age?

Quantitative Modeling of Resource Exhaustion

Robert B. Gordon
Tjalling C. Koopmans
William D. Nordhaus
Brian J. Skinner

Harvard University Press
Cambridge, Massachusetts, and London, England   1987

Library of Congress Cataloging in Publication Data

Toward a new Iron Age?

  Bibliography: p.
  Includes index.
  1. Nonrenewable natural resources—Mathematical models.
2. Resource allocation—Mathematical models.
3. Copper industry and trade—Mathematical models.
I. Gordon, Robert B. (Robert Boyd), 1929-
HC59.T63   1987   333.8'5   86-22923
ISBN 0-674-89818-4 (alk. paper)

Preface

Concerns about the adequacy of the globe's endowment of natural resources date back to the early days of the Industrial Revolution. People asked then, and people continue to wonder, whether economic growth will exhaust our precious heritage of fuels and nonfuel minerals, whether our salad days are numbered. Will consumers in advanced industrial countries find our living standards declining precipitously as low-cost natural resources are depleted?

Each of the four authors had analyzed these questions more or less independently—in studies of materials and substitution, in analyses of the size and distribution of different mineral deposits, in mathematical investigations of resource allocation and the price mechanism, and in empirical studies of the efficient use of energy resources. It fell to Tjalling Koopmans, however, to attempt to draw together the four separate strands of inquiry into this joint, interdisciplinary study of *materials modeling*—the study of resources, substitution, technology, and allocation of exhaustible natural resources or materials.

A word on the scientific background will illustrate why a wide range of disciplines is required for the materials-modeling approach. Nonfuel resources fall into two broad categories—superabundant and geochemically scarce. Many chemical elements or compounds—aluminum, iron, silicon—are intrinsically so abundant in the earth's crust that they can be recovered at near today's cost for an indefinitely long period. The geochemically scarce materials, by contrast, are so limited that the low-cost resources will be (or have been) exhausted, and our economies must inevitably turn to much higher cost ores or to substitute materials or technologies. The scarce materials include copper, gold, lead, zinc, silver, and a host of other metals.

In order to understand better how a market economy might deal with impending exhaustion, we decided to concentrate on the allocation of the most widely used of the geochemically scarce metals, copper. We discovered that we needed to know not only about the distribution of copper in the earth, both as ores and as common rocks, but also about the recycling of copper and about the possibilities for using substitute materials. Also, we needed to construct an economic model that included these geologic and engineering constraints in an explicit way.

It became clear early in the project that much of the necessary information and modeling would require collection and analysis of a mountain of geologic and engineering data. In addition, we needed to develop an analytical framework in which to synthesize the disparate elements of resources and demand. The National Science Foundation generously supported much of this project, and the AMAX company provided support for clerical assistance. David Laster was our first aide-de-camp in keeping minutes and performing computations. The first stage of data collection was started with the help of Robert Ortega. Subsequently Harry Hummel carried this forward and did much of the labor involved in calculating reserves and substitution costs. Anne-Marie Lambert performed a number of the computer runs. During the last three years of the project, Noriyuki Goto was an essential member of the team in polishing the computer codes, tabulating material, and weeding out errors and inconsistencies. Carol Ann Phelps drew the illustrations; Irene Khaitman, Glena Ames, and Cynthia Sclafani also helped see the project through to completion.

We received valuable help in acquiring data concerning the uses of copper from the Copper Development Association and from many copper-using industries. C. E. Linkous of the General Electric Company, Eric Cole of U.S. Electrical Motors Division of Emerson Industries, and Felix Zweig of the Electrical Engineering Department at Yale all helped us with the calculations of substitution costs for electrical motors and generators. Arnold Marcus of the G & O Manufacturing Company and Charles Mackenzie answered our questions about copper and aluminum heat exchangers. Comments and questions from many colleagues at Yale have helped us recognize weaknesses in our arguments and obscurities in our exposition. We particularly would like to thank Herbert Scarf: both as colleague and as director of the Cowles Foundation he encouraged and counseled us throughout the study.

As a final word, we note that our "copper project" was virtually completed when our friend and colleague, Tjalling Koopmans, died in February 1985. Tjalling participated in the project from its conception up to the last t-crossing—he was a full and active participant in every sense. We deeply regret that he did not live to see the final fruits of our collaboration.

R. B. G.

W. D. N.

B. J. S.

Contents

Toward a New Iron Age?

1 Introduction

Few will quarrel with the statement by the eminent geologist T. S. Lovering (1969:110) that "rich mineral deposits are a nation's most valuable but ephemeral material possession." Realization of this fact has led many countries, heavily dependent upon mining and exporting their mineral and fuel resources, to rethink the course of their economic development. They know that the high levels of income arising from ephemeral resources are transient; once mined, these elements will not be replenished. Concerns about dependence upon nonrenewable resources lead many geologists and others to conclude that when low-cost fuels and minerals have been exhausted the process of economic growth will slow and a very different kind of society, perhaps with greatly reduced standards of living, will emerge (see particularly Meadows et al. 1970).

Geologists and others who hold this somber view do not deny that the economic growth of the last two centuries has run counter to this thesis. But two centuries, they claim, is a short span in human history. The industrial countries have been spending their patrimony of low-cost minerals and fuels; the inheritance has been squandered and is about to run out. As the industrial economies turn to more abundant resources, the cost of these alternatives will be so high that their use will assuredly drag down future economic growth.

Some would go further to argue that supplies of all resources are linked together. Fuels, food, chemicals, and metals form a chain in which production of each one depends rigidly upon the availability of the others (Pimental et al. 1973). If one resource in the interacting network becomes scarce, the availability of some or many others will be adversely affected. The weakest links in the chain have never been tested, but they are clearly metals—particularly those metals that have essential alloying, electrical, thermal, magnetic, mechanical, or chemical properties. True, only small amounts of these metals are required to process vast quantities of fuel, to cultivate great tracts of land, or to produce huge quantities of manufactured goods, but without them the key processes of an advanced economy could fail or become exceedingly difficult.

Not all metals are necessarily weak links. Geochemical studies show that the total amount of any given metal concentrated in recoverable ore deposits is approximately proportional to the total amount of that metal in the earth's crust (see McKelvey 1960, Erickson 1973, and Skinner 1976). The ore deposits of the major metallic constituents of the crust—iron, aluminum, magnesium, titanium, and silicon—are truly enormous. These metals, the geochemically abundant elements, are each present in the earth's crust in amounts of 0.1 percent by weight or more. Several other metals, such as manganese, barium, and vanadium, are also available in quite large amounts, but the ore deposits of the rest of the metals are so limited that for most the discovery rate of new deposits is now less than current production. These are the geochemically scarce elements, each present at levels below 0.1 percent by weight of the earth's crust: they include such common metals as copper, lead, and zinc. It is within this geochemically scarce group that resource shortages are first likely to appear.

Today's economy relies primarily on rich ores, but deposits of the geochemically scarce metals are like tiny plums in a huge pudding. Somewhere between 0.01 and 0.001 percent of the metal content of the earth's crust is all that is concentrated in mineral deposits, including low-grade ores; the rest is distributed through the crust at very low levels of concentration in common rocks. From examination of the distribution of metals in rock and ores, Singer (1977), Skinner (1979), and others have shown that continued production of geochemically scarce metals will inevitably involve steep increases in the amount of energy required as processors are forced to turn to lower-grade ores and eventually common rock to obtain them. An increase in extraction costs may occur gradually or stepwise; if it is stepwise, Singer suggests that some steps will probably be so large as to prevent further widespread use of some metals.

A different view is found among many economists, who draw conclusions from the role of minerals in the economic growth process rather than from the way the minerals occur in the ground. These economists point to historical examples of transitions from scarce to more abundant resources; to the possibility that similar transitions will arise in the future; and to the price mechanism, which provides a control device for efficiently managing such transitions. A number of economic studies (Barnett and Morse 1963, Nordhaus and Tobin 1972, Pearce and Rose 1975, and Smith 1979) show that in the past substitution of new technologies or materials occurred sufficiently rapidly for the real (that is, constant-dollar) price of raw materials to fall over the last century. If history is a guide to the future, new technologies and materials to replace scarce resources will come into use without major economic dislocations. The optimistic view holds that, after a short period of adjustment, technological improvements will overcome at low cost any shortages due to exhaustion of geochemically scarce metals. This view is eloquently stated by Barnett and Morse (1963:244): "The physical properties of the natural resource base impose a series of initial constraints on growth and progress of man-kind, but the resource spectrum undergoes kaleidoscopic changes through time. Continued enlargement of the scope of substitutability—the result of man's technological ingenuity and organizational wisdom—offers those who are nimble a multitude of opportunities for escape."

The study reported in this book is a step toward resolving the debate between geologists and economists. It is an analysis of the future use of one metal, copper, based on an economic model and on geologic and engineering data for the resources available and for the opportunities for substituting alternative materials. Limiting the study to one metal is itself a major simplification because of the close interrelationships in the uses of metals today. If one metal is in short supply and a second is employed to make good the shortage, the substitution may create a deficit in another quarter. Analysis of this sort of coupling is, however, beyond present economic modeling capability.

Most existing methods for assessing resource availability use either short-run models—focusing no more than twenty years into the future—or very long run models. In the first category we find predominantly economic studies of resource markets, such as those by Fisher, Cootner, and Baily (1972), Arthur D. Little, Inc. (1978), and Mikesell (1979). For estimates of demand, such studies have generally relied on econometric (or behavioral) projections of both substitution possibilities and the responses of demand to income and prices. For the supply side, analysts have examined the nature of the capital stock and material inputs for production, but they have given little attention to the distribution and accessibility of geologic resources and, thus, to the long-run costs of extraction. Short-run studies are of great importance in addressing a number of immediate questions, such as short-term predictions of prices, imports, and environmental effects, but they shed no light on the long-run depletion patterns that are likely to come about over a period of decades. There are only a few long-run studies of materials markets—see especially Barnett and Morse (1963), Charles River Associates (1970, 1978), Fisher, Cootner, and Baily (1972), Hibbard et al. (1977), Pearce and Rose (1975), and Vogeley (1975).

One of the earliest works in resource economics was an 1866 study entitled *The Coal Question* by the eminent British economist William Stanley Jevons. Jevons showed a keen appreciation of the importance of resources when he declaimed, "Day by day it becomes more evident that the Coal we happily possess in excellent quality and abundance is the mainspring of modern material civilization." He reviewed resources and consumption patterns and then issued a somber warning concerning the impact of coal's depletion on the future growth of the British economy (for a recent reappraisal of Jevons's study, see Olby 1982).

After World War II the Paley commission (1952) reviewed the economic role of a number of resources and projected their availability, although these projections in many cases later proved to be wide of the mark (see Cooper 1975). A study by Tilton (1977) provided a balanced overview of the economic and policy issues for nonfuel minerals, but little new evidence on resources or demand patterns was developed.

In another early study, Herfindahl (1959) examined the behavior of copper prices over the period from 1870 to 1957 and concluded that there had been no significant rise in the deflated price of copper. Herfindahl's impressive work is largely historical and behaviorally oriented and pays scant attention to the potential future exhaustion of copper resources or to the process of substitution of other materials for copper.

Previous studies provide valuable information on many aspects of the economics of nonfuel minerals, but most devote little attention to the details of resource depletion and substitution. For instance, we are not aware of any studies that systematically examine the long-run substitution of other materials for copper—or, for that matter, for silver, zinc, helium, or gold. Neither do existing studies evaluate alternative processes that may replace the services of these materials. Nor have we encountered attempts to incorporate into materials studies engineering estimates of the future possibilities for recycling. Similar gaps exist with respect to development of new processes for the extraction of low-grade ores. It is just these details that will turn out, in the end, to be critical to the role of resources in long-run economic growth. This study attempts to fill an intellectual niche by studying the geology, substitution, and recycling patterns for the case of copper.

Choice of Copper

We chose copper for this study because it is one of the most important of
the geochemically scarce metals used in industrial economies. It appears in
a wide variety of products, and there are extensive data on its resources
and on the materials that can be used as substitutes for it. Its importance is
shown by the data on the cumulative world production of nonferrous
metals in Figure 1.1; only aluminum (a geochemically abundant metal) has
been produced in larger quantities. It is interesting to note that the last forty
years account for most of copper's cumulative production.

Experience accumulated in the search for ores provides a basis for assessing the grade, size, and accessibility of mineral deposits. Copper was
the first metal humans learned to smelt, and in time copper metallurgy was
developed by indigenous peoples on all the continents except Australia.
Large numbers of copper deposits, ranging from small veins of very rich
ore to enormous open-pit mines of lean ore, have been discovered and
mined over the past five thousand years. Data from all these mining ven-
tures provide part of the basis for assessing the distribution and metal
content of copper resources needed for our calculations. Potential short-

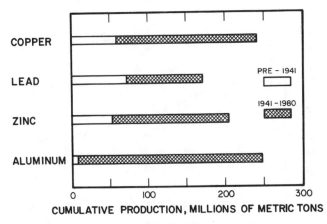

Figure 1.1 Cumulative worldwide production of the primary metals over all time.
The amounts produced since 1941 are shown by the shaded portions of each bar.
Although copper was the first metal to be smelted, more copper has been produced
since 1941 than in all the years before that time. (Reprinted with permission from
Journal of Metals 35, no. 5, 1983, a publication of the Metallurgical Society, War-
rendale, Pennsylvania.)

ages might be easier to predict for metals, such as tungsten or tantalum, that have been found in only a few localities and offer a relatively limited number of uses, but because of insufficient experience with different deposits of these metals we cannot forecast their availability over a period of a hundred years or more. Forecasts can be made with more confidence for copper than for any of the other geochemically scarce metals.

Many believe that the world faces severe copper shortages, or at least dramatic changes in supply patterns over coming decades. One reason that supply shifts are thought likely within the next fifty years is that the yield from copper ores in the United States has been steadily declining, as shown in Figure 1.2. Although the price of copper has been depressed recently because of weak demand and distress sales by developing countries, evidence suggests that the cost of copper, expressed in constant dollars, has been increasing since 1930, after having declined for many years (Peterson and Maxwell 1983). Because of the relative scarcity of copper, less expensive substitute materials, such as the copper-plated zinc now used for the U.S. penny, are appearing in products that were formerly made of copper.

Copper has a wide variety of uses, but more abundant materials can always be substituted for it. Copper and aluminum have been competitive materials in some applications, such as automobile radiators, for years; in

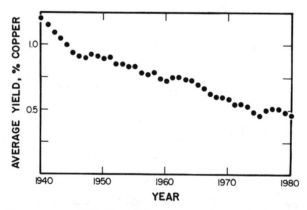

Figure 1.2 The average yield of metal from copper ores mined and smelted in the United States from 1940 to 1980. Yield is defined as the average grade of ore mined (expressed as the percentage of copper metal it contains) times the fraction of the contained copper that is recovered in smelting. (Reprinted with permission from *Journal of Metals* 35, no. 5, 1983, a publication of the Metallurgical Society, Warrendale, Pennsylvania.)

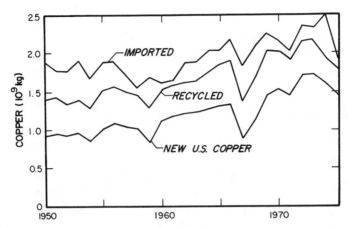

Figure 1.3 The sources of the copper metal used in the United States in recent years. Throughout this time period, newly smelted metal has been the dominant source of copper. (Data from *Mining and Minerals Policy, 1977,* Annual Report of the Secretary of the Interior, Washington, D.C., 1977.)

other applications zinc, plastics, stainless steel, or glass may replace copper. The cost of using substitutes for copper can be estimated more reliably than for other metals because of experience gained over a long period of competition between copper and other materials. Another advantage for our study is that substitution may occur in so many different products that a poor estimate for one application will not do as much damage to the model as for a metal that has only a few important uses. Copper has been recycled for many years, and data on this important component of the model, although less extensive than on substitution, are available.

The model is confined to the production and consumption of copper in the United States, because data on copper resources and use, both of which are required for the computations, are of poor quality for many countries outside North America; a model using worldwide but unreliable data would not yield results as dependable as one confined to the United States. Figure 1.3 shows that domestic production of new metal and recycling of old copper-containing products have met most of the demand for copper in the United States for many years.

Imports have recently gained a significant share of the U.S. market, however. Many copper-producing countries find it necessary to sell copper at or below average production cost to earn foreign exchange in today's depressed global economy. The high exchange rate on the dollar also helped foreign producers in the early and mid-1980s. A more normal pattern of global output and exchange rates would probably see the United States once again self-sufficient in copper. Hence a model limited to the United States does represent a realistic statement of the use of copper resources.

Analytical Issues in Materials Modeling

We move now to a thumbnail description of the modeling approach we shall follow, then briefly discuss the nature of our projections. In the final section we describe the relationship between our modeling exercise and the functioning of competitive markets, developing a simple example to show how the modeling technique operates.

We start with the observation that copper is a member of the class of geochemically scarce ores. Historically, the mined copper ores have been drawn from relatively rich deposits, averaging better than 1 percent copper metal. But the copper content ("grade") of minable ores has declined over the last century. Moreover, there is a geochemical limit to the availability of poorer grades of copper; below a certain threshold grade, copper occurs only in common rock, not as ore but in a very dilute solution. Happily, rock containing copper in solid solution is superabundant (available in quantities millions of times today's demand). Unhappily, the energy and other costs required to extract copper from common rock is many times greater than the cost of extracting copper from ores being mined today.

The prospect of mining extremely low-grade ores to maintain an advanced industrial society is the subject of this study. What will be the economic effect of making a transition to high-cost, low-grade ores? Will such a transition have a major impact on the living standards of future generations? What substitution patterns will occur as the transition period takes place?

To answer these questions we ask how the wide range of needs now served by copper (we call these "copper services") will be met in the future. These needs (electricity transmission, heat exchange, telecommunications, and coinage, to name but four) can be met by capital goods containing copper (wire, radiators, cables, and quarters); or they can be met by alternative materials and technologies (such as aluminum radiators, communications satellites, and credit cards). How much will it cost our economy to make the transition from today's low-cost, copper-based economy to tomorrow's alternatives? We begin to answer this question by identifying the important copper services (such as electricity transmission); we then list the resources and extraction costs of copper in the ground; we add the possibility of recycling old copper; and we identify substitute materials and processes that can meet the required copper services. Using these as the raw materials, we ask what is the most efficient way of providing the required copper services over time, whether it be by mining high-cost copper, by recycling copper, or by switching to alternative materials or processes. In the end we obtain an estimate of the efficient use, exhaustion, and pricing of copper, along with an estimate of the timing, patterns, and economic costs of substitution of alternative materials, over the next century and beyond.

The Nature of the Projections

At first blush the idea of projecting copper price and use patterns into the next century must seem foolhardy beyond belief. This impression would be reinforced if our results were seen as a forecast of future events. To prevent misunderstanding, we emphasize that we are not predicting the future. Rather, we are making a number of "if . . . then . . ." statements. Each projection is qualified by an explicit set of assumptions, and the conclusions or projections follow mathematically from these assumptions.

More specifically, we make explicit assumptions, based on the best available information, about resource availabilities, demand patterns, recycling possibilities, and so forth. We assume a certain market and informational structure. We add certain assumptions about discounting future costs and about the nature of technological advance. *Our projections follow from, and are conditional upon, the set of assumptions built into the economic model.* Clearly, then, the projections are no better or worse than are the assumptions that form the model's premises.

An Illustrative Copper-Aluminum Model

In the balance of this chapter we will develop a small model designed to illustrate the way our model operates and the nature of the results. This model should be studied by those who wish to understand the way the raw data are transformed into the projections that follow.

Assumptions of the illustrative model. In what follows we make the following assumptions:

1. We consider a model in which there are only two metals, copper and aluminum. Each is produced from inputs of ore of one concentration,

labor, and capital. One pound of each metal can produce one unit of "copper service," say, so many telephone calls. Copper is limited in supply, whereas aluminum is available in unlimited quantities.

2. We introduce the concept of competitive markets, with both spot and futures markets available for each metal.

3. We show the correspondence between our model of the metals and a competitive market for the two metals. We further discuss how the outcome of the competitive markets is the same as the solution of a simple optimization technique known as "linear programming" (LP).

4. We present the solution of the linear-programming problem for our simple copper-aluminum model, which also represents the outcome of competitive markets.

5. Finally, we define the nature of present-value prices and efficiency prices that, through the market mechanism, can induce the efficient rates of extraction and use of resources in different periods.

Extraction and use of the two metals. In the illustrative example we assume that aluminum ore is unlimited, whereas only 1,500 billion (1,500 × 10^9) pounds of copper are available for extraction in the entire future. (Note that we follow American usage of a billion to denote 1,000,000,000, or 10^9.) All this copper is assumed to have an extraction cost of $1.00 per pound expressed in constant dollars (that is, in dollars corrected for inflation).

We pretend that aluminum can serve as a substitute for copper, pound for pound, in all uses. The pertinent cost figure for any such use of aluminum, then, is the *sum* of the cost of extraction of one pound of aluminum and the extra cost, per pound of copper replaced, of producing and using the appropriate aluminum device over and above the cost of the copper product it replaced. For our model this number has been set at $6.00 per pound of copper replaced (hence also per pound of aluminum substituted); that $6.00 holds regardless of the particular use of copper for which aluminum is substituted. Recall that for simplicity we assume every service obtained from copper can be shifted to aluminum. We use the term "copper services" whether the services are rendered by devices made of copper *or* aluminum.

Spot and futures markets. We now imagine that the future is subdivided into a sequence of periods of 25 years each. At the beginning of each period a market in copper is held that looks ahead for as many periods as will be necessary to allocate supplies. With regard to the demand side of the market, it is postulated that for each time period total demand for copper services adds up to the equivalent of 13 billion pounds per year, implying a flow of 325 billion pounds (of copper plus aluminum) per 25-year period for the indefinite future. These demands are independent of the prices charged—an extreme case usually described as perfectly price-inelastic demand.

Since copper services can also be provided by aluminum, we assume a similar idealized market for aluminum at the beginning of each period. For simplicity we ignore all uses of aluminum for purposes other than copper services. The relative shares of copper and of aluminum in meeting the demand for copper services in each period are determined by the operation of the markets or, equivalently (as we shall see below), by the optimization calculated by linear programming.

In the market interpretation we assume that production and other activities are carried out at constant rates throughout each period. The industries producing and/or using the two metals are assumed to consist of perfectly competitive firms, which means that the firms do not collude and each is too small to affect market prices.

All firms and resource owners aim to maximize their own total discounted profits. That is, profits are made comparable with those in the first period by discounting the profit in the tth period through multiplication by a "discount factor," in our illustration set at 0.1^{t-1}. (This discount factor corresponds to an assumed real rate of return on investment of capital of about 9.5 percent per annum, because $1.095^{25} = 10$.) The rationale for this procedure is that in an economy with a capital market any prudent investment of a sum of dollars will, with reinvestment of all returns, grow at the same annual rate, here put at 9.5 percent (this assumes we disregard risk). We are always thinking in terms of *real* dollars, dollars of constant purchasing power. (For further explanations of this procedure, see Koopmans 1973, Lind 1982, and Nordhaus 1979.)

Again, the above description is not intended as a realistic and accurate model of resource allocation. Price and output fluctuations in the copper market occur daily, even hourly, not just once every 25 years. Costs seldom remain constant over time. There are no unique grades of copper and aluminum ores, as we have assumed, but many different grades of both ores. We have not allowed for unpredictable events, such as mine collapses, wars and revolutions, strikes, and import restrictions. Aluminum is not really a perfect substitute for copper, which means that additional costs derive from its use. Our $6.00-per-pound cost allowance for the production and use of aluminum is a rough attempt to cope with this complication. Finally, we have entirely ignored recycling in this example.

We have neglected all these realistic features of copper markets in the interest of first getting off the ground. In later chapters many realistic features will be explicitly incorporated into our more complex model.

Adam Smith corroborated by linear programming. We have just described a competitive general-equilibrium model, a mathematical representation of a hypothetical economy. In the case considered here, the model includes certain specific assumptions about the nature of consumers' demands for copper services; and it incorporates specific information, about geologic and engineering conditions, that permits calculation of the costs of production of the different metals. By combining all this information, the general-equilibrium model will generate estimates of (1) the total *quantities* of the two metals to be produced and used in each period so that consumers' requirements are met at lowest discounted costs, but always respecting technological, resource, and engineering constraints; and (2) the constant-dollar *prices* of these goods and services, where these prices are just appropriate to induce producers to provide the required quantities at the proper times.

A number of background assumptions are necessary to guarantee that the competitive markets will function properly, or indeed that they will exist. These assumptions include the absence of significant "increasing returns to scale," a term denoting the possibility that outputs increase more than proportionately to a balanced increase of inputs. We also must rule out effective collusion among firms or consumers and the possibility that informational deficiencies or transaction costs might lead to a breakdown of the competitive markets.[1]

But here we are only peripherally concerned with the technicalities of general-equilibrium theories. Rather, we wish to point to a relationship between competitive markets and linear programming. Linear-programming (LP) models minimize a given linear objective (such as costs) subject to a number of linear constraints or inequalities. In this study we rely extensively on LP models, which we discuss later in this chapter and in Chapter 4, to analyze patterns of copper exhaustion.

Why do we introduce LP analysis here? We do so because, under certain simplifying assumptions, we encounter a mathematical theorem of great economic importance: *the solution of a general economic equilibrium implicitly solves a cost-minimization problem that can be expressed in linear-programming form.* Surprisingly, we can determine the outcome of a general economic equilibrium by solving the linear-programming problem that is embedded in that equilibrium.

We can apply this result to our problem of exhaustible resources as follows: if each mining firm is faced with the same market prices for its inputs and outputs, and if each firm chooses its activities so as to maximize the firm's discounted profits, then the outcome will be economically efficient. In more precise language, such an equilibrium will be economically efficient in the sense that (1) each firm will provide its share of the market at minimum discounted cost; and (2) the requirements of the market (for copper and other kinds of services) will be met by producers in a manner that satisfies total demand at minimum discounted total cost to society.

Examining these two conditions, we see that our competitive equilibrium has indeed solved a minimization problem of sorts—it has found a way of providing the appropriate array of services at lowest possible costs. But this minimization is exactly the objective of a linear-programming problem as well; an LP problem typically attempts to minimize the costs of performing some set of activities subject to a number of linear inequalities. Consequently, we can mimic the outcome of the economic equilibrium by solving the LP problem that minimizes the same set of cost functions subject to the same set of technical constraints. Put differently, given the appropriate quantities of resources available and the proper demand requirements, by solving a cost-minimizing LP problem we can determine the equilibrium market prices and quantities for copper and other magnitudes for all future periods. We call this lucky analytical coincidence the correspondence principle: *determining the prices and quantities in a general economic equilibrium and solving the embedded cost-minimization problem by linear programming are mathematically equivalent.*[2]

The correspondence principle echoes one of the earliest ideas of the classical economists, that of the invisible-hand principle pronounced by Adam Smith in 1776. Smith asserted that although each individual pursues only his own gain he promotes the interests of society as if led "by an invisible hand." The correspondence principle is indeed a rigorous statement of the invisible-hand principle whereby, in our example, a competitive equilibrium allocation will generate a time path of prices and quantities that provides copper services at minimal discounted cost to society.

The linear-programming problem. Having given the correspondence principle, we next lay out the LP problem that mimics the competitive equilibrium for our simple copper-aluminum example. In brief, the LP problem is to minimize the total discounted costs subject to the constraints that total copper extracted be within the available resources and that the demand requirements be met.

Begin with the cost minimization. We denote by C_t the total extraction and use of copper in period t, and by A_t the extraction and use of aluminum in period t (both quantities and total costs are in billions). Our LP problem is to minimize the discounted cost of copper and aluminum use, which is calculated over a span of six periods. We thus minimize the following sum:

(1.1) $0.1^0(C_1 + 6A_1) + 0.1^1(C_2 + 6A_2) + \ldots + 0.1^5(C_6 + 6A_6).$

Here 0.1^t represents the discount factor applied to the different cost terms in period $(t + 1)$. This sum of costs, sometimes called the objective function, is to be minimized subject to two sets of constraints. The first constraint is that the total amount of copper mined cannot exceed the amount available for extraction, 1,500 billion pounds. Hence

(1.2) $C_1 + C_2 + C_3 + C_4 + C_5 + C_6 \leq 1{,}500.$

Second, in each period the total production of copper services (whether by copper or by aluminum) must be at least as great as the demand requirement, 325 billion pounds:

(1.3) $C_t + A_t \geq 325, \quad t = 1, \ldots, 6.$

Additionally, we cannot allow negative production levels, so both C_t and A_t are nonnegative. Finally, we have implicitly included an assumption of additivity, or constant returns to scale, in production. By this we mean that a doubling of all inputs will lead to a doubling of output (and similarly for any positive multiple of each process).

Finding values of C_t and A_t that minimize the sum in Expression (1.1) is equivalent to selecting a schedule of copper and aluminum production that will incur the lowest total discounted cost of extraction and use over the next 150 years. It is just the solution to this LP problem that corresponds to the outcome of competitive markets.

Optimal production and pricing. We have constructed a problem sufficiently simple that the least-cost or "optimal" solution can be guessed. In all periods the extraction and use of copper is much cheaper than that of an equivalent amount of its substitute, aluminum. Moreover, because of the economic motive to postpone costs, as represented by the discount factor less than unity, it will be efficient to use the less expensive material (copper) before the more expensive material (aluminum). This reasoning suggests that the market will rely completely on copper in the early periods and shift to aluminum when copper is exhausted.

Table 1.1 Optimal extraction of copper and aluminum in successive 25-year periods

Period	Amounts extracted and used (billions of pounds)		Discounted cost of optimal program (billions of discounted $)
	Copper	Aluminum	
1	325	0	325.0
2	325	0	32.5
3	325	0	3.25
4	325	0	0.325
5	200	125	0.095
6	0	325	0.0195
Total for all periods	1,500	450	361.1895

The optimal pattern of resource use—to use the least expensive resource as long as it lasts and then turn to more expensive and more abundant resources later in time—is shown in Table 1.1. The quantities of aluminum and copper extraction provided in the table, along with the discounted costs shown in the last column, do indeed minimize the discounted costs summed in Expression (1.1). In this optimal or least-cost pattern copper alone is employed through the fourth period; copper and aluminum together are used in the fifth period; then from the sixth period on, after copper is exhausted, aluminum alone remains to be drawn upon for meeting demand requirements.

This intuitive analysis (which will shortly be made more rigorous) also indicates why we need to consider only six periods in our simple copper-aluminum example. The minimum-cost solution for the first six periods would have been the same if we had included eight or ten or a hundred periods in the summed costs in equation (1.1). In the last case, the solution would have been the same as in Table 1.1 for the first six periods, after which we would have the following sequence:

$$C_7 = C_8 = \ldots = C_{100} = 0; \qquad A_7 = A_8 = \ldots = A_{100} = 325.$$

That is, copper services would be supplied entirely by aluminum after the sixth period, and no decisions in the first six periods would be affected by an additional string of periods to consider. Hence we need consider a time horizon only as long as the scarce resource is being used.

Dual variables and efficiency prices. Although the argument of the last section is intuitively appealing, we will confirm the results by developing the concept of efficiency prices. This concept will prepare for the more detailed discussion and application in Chapters 4 and 5.

Recall that we are using our simple copper-aluminum model to illustrate the correspondence between linear programming and a highly idealized set of competitive markets. We first set the stage for a more complete analysis by describing the idealized competitive market for our copper-aluminum model.

We contemplate a fictitious market in which all transactions occur at the beginning of the first period—an economic analogue to the physicists' primordial big bang taking place at time zero. At this initial time all future prices, costs, and production rates are calculated, and transactions are made on an extensive set of spot and futures markets for copper and aluminum. Of course, such a process does not occur in reality; but this idealized view of general economic equilibrium allows us to be assured that all future extraction, production, and consumption decisions are efficiently and consistently made.

In order to make their calculations producers and consumers need to know current and future costs and prices. To see why, focus on firms that are assumed to maximize the discounted value of their profits. Each firm will need to calculate the costs and revenues associated with extracting, refining, and selling copper and aluminum in different periods. A firm might, for example, decide to buy copper resources-in-the-ground in period 2 and extract and sell these in period 4. To assure itself that such an activity would maximize its profits, the firm would need to know the prices reigning in each period. In making these kinds of cost and profit calculations, firms need to possess the competitive market prices for each material in each future period.

What is the analogue of the competitive market price in our LP model? It is the present-value price (sometimes called the "dual variable," which we discuss more extensively at the end of this chapter). Present-value prices are those values that, when used by producers and consumers to make their consumption and production decisions, lead to allocations of scarce resources in the least-cost or most efficient manner. That is, the profit-maximizing responses of individual producers to these prices will actually provide the same results as that of the LP solution. Present-value prices are

so central to our calculations that we will discuss their meaning and deriva-
tion before we proceed further.

The present-value price appears bizarre to those familiar with the prices
quoted in stores or newspapers. It represents the price *paid today* for
quantities delivered in the future. Put differently, it is the value of future
prices in today's dollars; it corrects the actual values that will occur in the
future for the effect of discounting over the intervening period.

For example, assume that the nominal or money interest rate is 9.5
percent per annum and that we are paying in 1990 for copper that will be
delivered in 2015 at a current-value price of 131.7 cents per pound. (A
current-value price is the actual price that will be paid for future transactions at that future date.) Because the discount factor is 0.10 for 25 years,
the present-value price for this transaction will be 13.17 cents per pound.
That is, if we pay for our 2015 copper in 1990, we will need to pay only
13.17 cents a pound because of the interest that will be earned over the 25
years, this compound interest allowing the 13.17 cents to grow to 131.7
cents in 2015. In this example, then, the present-value price for 2015 copper
in 1990 will be 13.17 cents; more generally, the present-value price is the
current-value price discounted back to the present. More precisely, let us
define the following present-value prices:

w = present-value price of copper ore, or copper-in-the-ground, hereafter called "copper ore price" (we shall see below that w has no time
subscript);

u_t = present-value price of one pound of copper metal (after extraction
and refining) in period t, hereafter called "copper metal price";

v_t = present-value price of aluminum (after extraction and processing) in
period t, hereafter called "aluminum price."

We show in Table 1.2 the calculated present-value prices for our simple
copper-aluminum model. Note first that the present-value price of copper
ore is the same for all periods, because the market price of copper ore,
requiring no labor or capital to lie undisturbed under the soil, will rise at the
discount rate or interest rate in an efficient allocation. Hence, in present-
value terms, the price of ore remains constant over time.

Next, note that the present-value prices for copper metal extend only
through period 5, for after that time there is no more copper remaining and
its price is purely fictitious. Also, the present-value prices of copper metal
decline sharply over time, starting at $1.0005 per pound in the first period

Table 1.2 Present value prices for copper and aluminum in the optimal program

Period	Present-value prices (in discounted dollars per pound)	
	Copper[a]	Aluminum
1	$u_1 = w + 1.0 = 1.0005$	$v_1 \leqq 6.0$
2	$u_2 = w + 0.1 = 0.1005$	$v_2 \leqq 0.6$
3	$u_3 = w + 0.01 = 0.0105$	$v_3 \leqq 0.06$
4	$u_4 = w + 0.001 = 0.0015$	$v_4 \leqq 0.006$
5	$u_5 = w + 0.0001 = 0.0006$	$v_5 = 0.0006$
6	Copper exhausted	$v_6 = 0.00006$

a. w = present-value price of copper ore for all periods = 0.0005.

and ending at $0.0006 per pound in the fifth period. Of course, the actual market prices do not decline that sharply; it is the force of discounting future prices that renders so tiny the present-value prices of distant events.

The present-value prices of aluminum are expressed in terms of inequalities for the first four periods and as equalities from the fifth period on. The inequalities through period 4 signify that market participants are willing to pay less than the costs of production for aluminum, so there is no production. In the fifth period, the first period in which aluminum is used, the present-value price is $0.0006 per pound (or the constant-dollar price of $6 times the discount factor of 0.0001).

Once we have calculated the present-value prices it is relatively simple to compute the efficiency prices. By efficiency prices we mean the present-value prices converted into the values that will prevail on the date on which quantities are actually produced, shipped, and used. In trading terminology, they are the spot prices at which goods change hands. Note that the efficiency prices are similar to present-value prices in that they reflect prices such that if producers and consumers make consumption and production decisions on their basis, society will allocate resources in an efficient manner. The only difference between present-value prices and efficiency prices is the unit of measurement, not the economic interpretation. In symbols, we set

z_t = efficiency price of copper ore in period t;

p_t = efficiency price of copper metal in period t;

q_t = efficiency price of aluminum in period t.

To compute efficiency prices we simply undo the discounting calculation performed on p. 17. That is, if the present-value price for deliveries 25 years hence is 13.17 cents per pound, and if the 25-year discount factor is 0.1, then the efficiency price is 131.7 cents per pound.

Table 1.3 shows the efficiency prices that correspond to the present-value prices shown in Table 1.2. It shows that the efficiency price for copper metal rises over time until, in the fifth period, copper metal and aluminum have equal prices, after which copper is exhausted. Note as well that the efficiency price of copper ore rises by a factor of ten each quarter-century (or at 9.5 percent per annum) until copper is exhausted.

Analytical aspects of the calculations. In this section we pursue in further detail the approach of LP and the correspondence principle to show why the pattern of results of Tables 1.1 through 1.3 arises and to explain the methods of LP calculations. To begin we observe that, in a competitive market in economic equilibrium, the prices of all inputs and outputs must produce a net profit on each activity that is either zero (for processes that are in use) or negative (for processes that are not in use). "Profits" are here used in a very broad sense, not in the way customarily encountered in accounting statements; here profits denote all revenues minus all costs, including the opportunity costs of scarce factors, such as capital, patents, and entrepreneurship, owned by firms.

Why must viable processes yield zero profits? Economic forces rule out both positive and negative profits for economic processes that are in use. Positive profits are ruled out because, if revenues minus costs for a process were greater than zero, firms would expand production and drive down the price until the process was no longer profitable. Conversely, negative profits would induce firms to leave the market, causing production to de-

Table 1.3   Efficiency prices for copper and aluminum in the optimal program

Period	Copper ore	Efficiency prices (in constant dollars per pound) Copper metal	Aluminum
1	$z_1 = 0.0005$	$p_1 = w + 1.0 = 1.0005$	$q_1 \leqq 6.0$
2	$z_2 = 0.005$	$p_2 = 10(w + 0.1) = 1.005$	$q_2 \leqq 6.0$
3	$z_3 = 0.05$	$p_3 = 100(w + 0.01) = 1.05$	$q_3 \leqq 6.0$
4	$z_4 = 0.5$	$p_4 = 1{,}000(w + 0.001) = 1.5$	$q_4 \leqq 6.0$
5	$z_5 = 5.0$	$p_5 = 10{,}000(w + 0.0001) = 6.0$	$q_5 = 6.0$
6		Copper exhausted	$q_6 = 6.0$

Table 1.4   Calculation of present-value prices using the zero-profit condition

Period in which copper is mined and used	Zero-profit condition	Present-value prices
1	$-1\ w + 1\ u_1 - 1\ \ \ \ = 0$	$u_1 = w + 1$
2	$-1\ w + 1\ u_2 - 10^{-1} = 0$	$u_2 = w + 10^{-1}$
3	$-1\ w + 1\ u_3 - 10^{-2} = 0$	$u_3 = w + 10^{-2}$
4	$-1\ w + 1\ u_4 - 10^{-3} = 0$	$u_4 = w + 10^{-3}$
5	$-1\ w + 1\ u_5 - 10^{-4} = 0$	$u_5 = w + 10^{-4}$

cline until the price had risen to the point where profits were back to zero. Note that the zero-profit condition is a result of our competitive market, not an assumption of this particular market.

Once we admit the zero-profit condition, it is straightforward to calculate the prices in our simple copper-aluminum example. This calculation is shown in Table 1.4 for the processes which, from our earlier discussion, we suspect to be the optimal activities in the first five periods—these processes being the extraction and use of copper in the first five periods.

Note that numerical values can be inserted for u_t, the present-value prices for copper metal, as soon as the intriguing and crucial variable w, the present-value price of copper ore, has been determined.[3]

What then is this crucial variable w, the price of copper ore? For an interpretation, we rely upon the "dual problem" in linear programming. In the dual, the present-value price of a variable (or, technically, the dual variable or shadow price)[4] represents the contribution of that variable—be it labor, land, capital, oil, or mineral ore—to the society's net economic output. More precisely, the value w represents the amount that an extra unit of copper resource-in-the-ground would reduce the total discounted cost of meeting society's copper requirements.

To see how we might calculate the actual value of w, we make a "small" change in the total amount of available copper, say, from 1,500 to 1,501 billion pounds. We proceed to solve the cost-minimizing LP problem once more, changing the copper availability from 1,500 to 1,501 units but leaving all other parameters the same. The present-value price of copper metal is then equal to—and can indeed be defined as—the saving in total discounted cost due to the one-unit increase in available copper resources.[5]

The actual calculation for the present-value price of copper ore is shown in Table 1.5. Here we compare the original solution shown in Tables 1.1 to

Table 1.5 Illustrative calculation of the present-value price of copper-in-the-ground

	Unit	Variables subjected to change		Availability of copper	Total cost saving due to modification
		C_5	A_5		
Least-cost amount					
In original program	10^9 lb	200	125	1,500	
In modified program	10^9 lb	201	124	1,501	
Modification	10^9 lb	1	-1	1	
Cost coefficient	$ per lb	10^{-4}	6×10^{-4}		
Net effect of modification on discounted cost	(10^9) per 10^9 lb	10^{-4}	-6×10^{-4}		$w = 5 \times 10^{-4}$

Note: C_5 and A_5 are, respectively, the production of copper and aluminum in period 5.

1.4 with a modified solution that adds the one additional unit of copper ore. By working through Table 1.5, we find the saving in discounted cost to be \$0.0005 per additional pound of copper ore. We have therefore discovered our important present-value price for copper ore, $w = \$0.0005$, in our simple example.

One technical note should be added about this calculation: our definition of w remains valid regardless of the precise choice of the "small" unit as long as the net addition to the total availability of copper is not so large as to require a change in the processes or activities used. If, for example, the increment to resources were enough to allow copper production to extend into the sixth period (say an increment of 300 billion pounds), then the activities would change and the calculation would be incorrect. Further note that w is a price—that is, a sum of money divided by a quantity, here expressed in billions of dollars divided by billions of pounds of copper.

Now that we have determined the value of w, we can compute the values of all other present-value prices by using the equations in the last column of Table 1.4. In these the crucial zero-profit condition along with the present-value price of copper ore allows us to calculate the present-value prices for copper metal in different periods. The end results are shown in Table 1.2.

Our remarks about copper can be applied to aluminum as well. The distinction between the two metals in our simple example is that the price for aluminum does not reflect resource scarcity; that is, if we were to define w^* as the present-value price of aluminum-in-the-ground, its value would be zero because aluminum is superabundant. Hence during the periods in which aluminum is produced, aluminum prices are equal to extraction and use costs alone (\$6 per pound, appropriately discounted) and include no term for resource scarcity.

Finally, it is useful to subdivide prices into two different terms, the *extraction cost* and the *royalty*.[6] Extraction costs have been previously defined. The royalty is just the price corresponding to the efficiency price of copper-in-the-ground. The division is set out in Table 1.6. The costs of extraction are shown at their assumed constant values. The royalty for copper grows sharply over time (in fact, as noted above, it grows at the rate of interest or discount rate) and is shown only through the fifth period, after which copper is exhausted. The total efficiency price of copper is simply the sum of the extraction cost and royalty.

Examine briefly the results for the fifth period, during which aluminum and copper are both used. We will later call this period a *switch point* because at this point there is a switch from copper to a substitute material.

Table 1.6 Royalty and extraction costs as components of efficiency prices[a]

Period (t)	Copper			Aluminum
	Total price	Royalty	Cost of extraction	Cost of extraction
1	1.0005	0.0005	1	6
2	1.005	0.005	1	6
3	1.05	0.05	1	6
4	1.5	0.5	1	6
5	6.0	5.0	1	6
6		Exhausted		6

a. All prices in constant dollars per pound.

At the switch point, aluminum and copper must have equal prices for equivalent services. In our example, copper and aluminum services must be priced at $6 per pound in period 5. This implies that the royalty for copper in period 5 is $5 per pound ($6 less $1 for extraction costs). We can then calculate the royalty for copper in earlier periods by applying the appropriate discount factors. The result of this calculation is shown in the third column of Table 1.6. Also note that aluminum does not have a positive royalty component because it is assumed to be superabundant; the efficiency price of aluminum is therefore always equal to $6—which is the extraction and use cost of $6 plus aluminum's royalty of $0.

We have now concluded the presentation of our simple model of the linear-programming and competitive-equilibrium approaches to the allocation of scarce mineral resources over time. This example is not constructed as a realistic, empirical basis for understanding the copper industry. Rather, like an architect's scaled-down model of a building, our copper-aluminum model is designed to give a conceptual overview of our later discussion. By understanding this relatively transparent example, we can better comprehend the methods used to calculate the efficient prices and quantities in the much more complex and realistic model that follows in the next five chapters. The key points to grasp here are the technique for calculating the quantities produced of copper and aluminum, the concepts of efficiency prices and royalties, and the crucial correspondence principle between LP calculations and competitive markets. The enormously more complex model that follows—with dozens of grades and demand categories, several substitute materials, and multiple recycling possibilities—is but an elaboration of the simple structure highlighted in the copper-aluminum model of this chapter.

In the remainder of this book, we flesh out the bare-bones model presented in this chapter. We first consider, in Chapters 2 and 3, issues of geology, substitution, recycling, and demand—thereby securing for our study a firm empirical base. Then, in Chapters 4 and 5, we turn to a complete analysis of the patterns of resource exhaustion, substitution, and the associated price paths, along with sensitivity analyses to account for uncertainties about crucial issues. Finally, in Chapter 6, we return to the broader terrain, the problem of resource depletion and economic growth, from which we launched the study.

2 Copper Resources

The exact amount of copper that will be won from the earth's crust cannot be known until mining ceases and the last gram has been extracted. Nor can future costs of mining and processing be stated exactly. Even so, it is possible to assess, within realistic limits, the magnitude of the copper resources that lie within any given volume of the earth's crust. Estimates are based on knowledge of the way copper is distributed through the rocks of the crust. Whether we humans will be clever enough to find all the ores that exist is an unanswerable question. But for the copper ores that are found, the cost of extracting and processing them can be estimated, within reasonable bounds, on the basis of the experiences of generations of miners and metallurgists. In this chapter we address the problem of estimating both the quantity and the costs of copper.

Copper Ores

How Copper Occurs in the Crust

The costs of mining and producing metallic copper depends in part on the way atoms of copper are bound in minerals. We need consider only the minerals in the crust of the earth. The crust is the outermost of earth's compositional layers, ranging in thickness from 10 kilometers beneath the oceans to 40 kilometers beneath continents. It is comprised of a large number of different kinds of rock, each of which contains at least traces of copper. The ease with which copper can be produced from a given rock is determined both by the amount of copper in a rock and by the way the copper is chemically bound to other atoms.

Rocks are aggregates of minerals. Most contain several kinds of minerals, two or three of which usually account for 90 percent or more of the mass of the rock. Minerals—discrete, solid, chemical compounds—are characterized by a specific chemical composition and a specific packing geometry of the constituent atoms. The packing geometry is called the crystal structure of the mineral. Although 3,000 different minerals have been identified, only 30 are major constituents in common rocks. Most of the rock-forming minerals are silicates, with the remainder being oxides, hydroxides, and carbonates, but in all cases the essential chemical elements of the rock-forming minerals are limited to a short list—oxygen, silicon, aluminum, iron, calcium, magnesium, sodium, potassium, titanium, manganese, hydrogen, and carbon. Indeed, more than 99 percent of the mass of the earth's crust is comprised of minerals containing two or more of these 12 superabundant elements. All the remaining chemical elements are present simply as low-level traces in the crust.

No rock-forming mineral contains copper as an essential chemical element. Instead, copper atoms are randomly distributed in tiny amounts in a state known as atomic substitution or, as it is often called, solid solution. In this state, atoms of one chemical element substitute for atoms of another in the crystal structure of a mineral, without altering the structure or significantly changing the chemical properties of the host. For example, copper atoms readily substitute for magnesium or iron atoms in minerals such as biotite, $KMg_3AlSi_3O_{10}(OH)_2$, and pyroxene, $FeSiO_3$, but do not change the properties of either mineral. A limit usually applies to the amount of an element that may combine in a solid solution, as in liquid solutions. And just as the solubility limits, or saturations, of liquid solutions are marked by the formation of crystals of the dissolved compound, so are the limits of a solid solution marked by the appearance of a new mineral when saturation is reached. When copper concentrations reach a level of about 0.1 percent of the mass of a mineral, the limit has been reached in most common minerals and individual copper minerals form (COMRATE 1975).

Because the copper content of the earth's crust is only 0.007 percent by weight, and because no common rocks are known to have copper contents approaching the 0.1 percent value, it is assumed that most of the copper in the crust is atomically locked up in dilute solid solutions. We draw an important conclusion from these facts: a copper concentration of about 0.1 percent marks a distinct *mineralogical barrier* separating common rocks from copper ores. Rocks that have more than 0.1 percent copper are observed to contain copper minerals, most of which are comprised of at least 30 percent copper. When copper minerals are present they can be freed from the enclosing mixture of valueless silicate minerals by crushing and grinding and can then be concentrated by a selective process such as flotation. The resulting concentrate of copper minerals, which are generally sulfide minerals, is smelted to prepare metallic copper. The process of mining and grinding copper ores, followed by preparation and then smelting of a concentrate, requires considerable energy, and the amount of energy required increases as the concentration of copper drops. Copper concentrations are commonly denoted by grades, expressed in copper's percent by weight of a given mineral or ore. More ore must be mined, crushed, separated and smelted at low grades than at high to prepare the same mass of copper.

At mineral concentrations below 0.1 percent, separation of individual copper minerals is impossible because all the copper is locked in solid solution in silicate minerals. In this case the silicate minerals themselves must be separated and smelted—a process that is energy intensive and expensive. The amount of energy needed to smelt a silicate mineral is much greater than that needed to smelt a sulfide mineral, because the chemical bonds holding the atoms together in a silicate mineral are much stronger than those holding atoms in a sulfide mineral. Indeed, metallurgical practice shows that at least ten times more energy is needed to process a silicate mineral than a sulfide. The energy difference accounts for the dramatic mineralogical barrier shown in Figure 2.1.

The feasibility of recovering copper from mineral deposits at concentrations above 0.1 percent depends on the grade, the size of the deposit, and

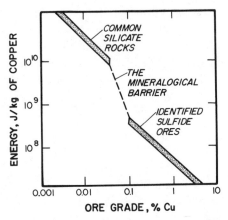

Figure 2.1 Energy required to recover copper from sulfide ores and by atomic substitution from common silicate minerals. The highest grades observed in common rocks do not overlap the lowest grades observed in ore deposits: the jump from the sulfide-ore curve to the silicate-rock curve is a mineralogical barrier that must someday be faced if copper is to be won from common rocks. (After Skinner 1979a.)

the depth of the deposit below the surface. At concentrations below 0.1 percent, the size and depth of the rock unit are less important because the rock could be taken from the earth's crust near the surface, presumably in great volume, but the amount of copper in the rock and the costs of metallurgical extraction become highly important. In assessing copper resources, therefore, we face two different groups of questions. First, we must ask how the copper is distributed through ore deposits and what are the grade, size, and depth of the deposits and the costs of extracting the copper from the ores. Second, we must ask which common rocks contain the most copper and what is the cost of recovering the copper. In this chapter we approach these questions in the same order. We begin with an examination of copper ores, then turn to the way they form, how large the deposits are, what their grades are, and how the deposits are distributed through the crust.

Copper Ores and Ore Minerals

Copper ore is a mixture of one or more copper minerals dispersed through a large volume of valueless minerals called the gangue. About a hundred copper minerals have been identified, but only six are important ore minerals (Table 2.1). Each of these is a sulfide compound, and far and away the most important so far as copper mining is concerned is chalcopyrite ($CuFeS_2$). Sulfide ore minerals of copper are rarely found in common rocks. Rather, they occur where some localized geological process has raised the concentration sufficiently to form one of the small rock masses we call ore bodies. The concentrating processes and the reasons deposits

Table 2.1   The important copper minerals

Mineral	Formula	Percentage of copper (by wt.)
Chalcopyrite	$CuFeS_2$	35
Bornite	Cu_5FeS_4	63
Digenite	Cu_9S_5	72
Chalcocite	Cu_2S	80
Tetrahedrite	$Cu_{12}Sb_4S_{13}$	46
Enargite	Cu_3AsS_4	48

are distributed the way they are throughout the crust are still subjects of research. Even so, enough is known of the processes for deposits to be classified and the classification used as a basis for estimating copper resources.

Copper ore bodies can be loosely classified as follows.

1. *Vein deposits*. Veins are tabular masses with sharp boundaries, in which ore minerals are confined to a fracture or opening in a valueless host rock (Fig. 2.2). They are formed by deposition from hot, copper-bearing solutions. The fluids, called hydrothermal solutions, can start as downward-percolating rainwater or upward-flowing solutions released by cooling magmas. Regardless of the source of hydrothermal solutions, their chemical properties vary little. When defined flow channels such as rock fractures are present, deposition from solution can fill the open space and form a vein. A good example of vein deposits are the famous ore bodies of Cornwall, England. The resulting ore bodies are frequently very rich, and for this reason they have in the past been important sources of copper, as well as of many other metals such as lead, zinc, tin, gold, and silver. Today vein deposits are quantitatively the least important class of copper ore bodies.

2. *Porphyry copper deposits*. Porphyry deposits are closely related to vein deposits in that they also are formed by circulating hydrothermal solutions. They form within and beneath stratovolcanoes—the steep-sided, often beautiful volcanic cones of which Mount Fuji and Mount Rainier are famous examples. The ores derive their name from the distinctive porphyritic texture of the igneous rocks that form the core of stratovolcanoes.

Volcanic processes in stratovolcanoes are commonly explosive. As a result of the explosions large volumes of rock are shattered to form an aquifer. Hydrothermal solutions circulate through the shattered mass (Fig. 2.3), and the entire rock mass becomes impregnated with innumerable tiny veinlets of ore minerals (Fig. 2.4). Only a millimeter or two wide and far too small to mine individually, the veinlets are often only a few centimeters apart, which means that the whole rock mass can be mined as a unit.

Most porphyry copper deposits discovered to date—like the deposits at Bingham Canyon, Utah, and Chuquicamata, Chile—are relatively young in a geological sense, less than 250 million years old. Their distribution is clearly related to the shape and present motion of tectonic plates, because the volcanoes in which they form are clustered along the edges of the plates

Figure 2.2   A vein deposit of copper minerals at Casapalca, Peru. The scale can be judged from the hat worn by the miner in the foreground.

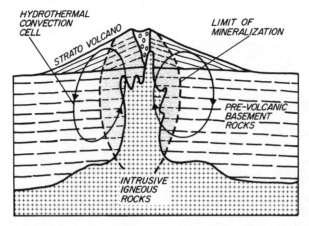

Figure 2.3 Hydrothermal circulation system forming a porphyry copper deposit beneath a stratovolcano.

(Fig. 2.5). It is presumed that older ore deposits were formed as a result of earlier plate motions.

3. *Massive sulfide ores.* When volcanism occurs beneath the sea, seawater penetrates the hot, porous, volcanic rock pile and convection cells develop within it. The heated seawater reacts with the rocks through which it passes and becomes a hydrothermal solution. When the rising limb of a convection cell returns the hydrothermal solution to the sea as a plume of hot water, the plume rapidly cools and deposits its dissolved load of ore and gangue minerals in a blanket around the vent (Fig. 2.6). Deposits formed in this manner are not necessarily large in size, but they are said to be "massive" because they consist largely of sulfide minerals, whereas quartz and other common gangue minerals are minor constituents.

Deep-diving research submarines have observed massive sulfide ores in the process of formation along the East Pacific Rise. The rise marks the join of two tectonic plates and is a site of active submarine volcanism, although a very different kind of volcanism from that which produces porphyry copper deposits. No doubt there are many sites still to be discovered around the world where massive sulfide deposits are forming.

4. *Stratabound deposits.* Fluids that fill spaces between grains in sedimentary rocks can become hydrothermal solutions. Such solutions are commonly encountered by oil-well drillers and have been known for many years, but only recently has it been recognized that they can form impor-

Figure 2.4   Veinlets of copper minerals laced through a shattered mass of altered igneous rock; a typical porphyry copper ore. The sample is from the Silver Bell deposit, Arizona. (Millimeter scale.)

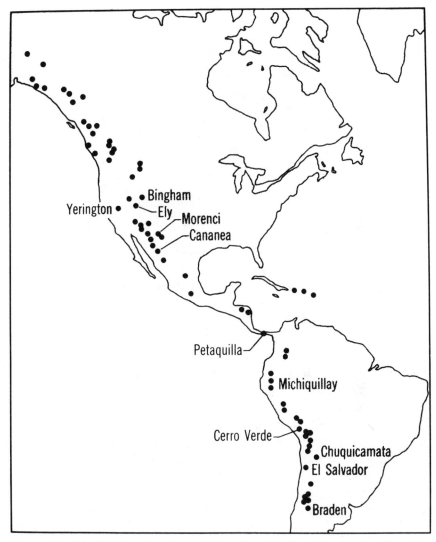

Figure 2.5 Distribution of porphyry copper deposits along the western edge of the Americas.

tant ore bodies (Fig. 2.7). The ores are found within specific, sedimentary strata, for which reason they are called stratabound. The processes that introduce the ore minerals may commence soon after a sedimentary layer is deposited, while the sediment is still a soft mud, or they may occur much later, after the layer has become rock. Regardless of the timing that pro-

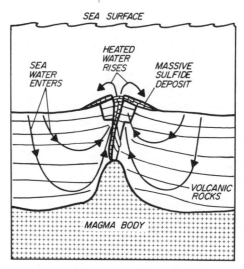

Figure 2.6   Massive sulfide deposit formed on the sea floor. The rising plume of a convection cell deposits sulfide minerals on and in volcanic rocks on the sea floor. Deposits of this kind have been observed forming today above the East Pacific Rise.

duces them, all stratabound deposits tend to be similar in form and feature in that they are confined to one or more favorable strata and they are found in shallow, near-shore sediments.

Stratiform deposits are important sources of lead and zinc as well as copper. Well-known examples are the great copper ores of Zambia, the Kupferschiefer of East Germany and Poland, and the White Pine deposits in Michigan.

5. *Magmatic segregation deposits.* This class of copper deposit does not require hydrothermal solutions but forms entirely by magmatic processes. Some magmas deep in the earth's mantle will, on rising and cooling in the crust, become saturated with iron sulfide. If the temperature of the magma is low, iron sulfide precipitates as crystals of pyrrhotite (FeS), but more commonly the precipitation occurs at such high temperatures (above 1,065°C) that the iron sulfide is molten. In this case a globule of liquid iron sulfide forms and, being more dense than silicate magma, sinks to the floor of the magma chamber, where it coalesces with other globules to form a molten sulfide layer. The iron sulfide liquid is never pure, because it contains a few percent of copper and/or nickel. When cooled and crystallized,

Figure 2.7. Stratabound ore formed by hydrothermal solutions expelled from deeper to shallower parts of a sedimentary basin. The dark bands are common silicate minerals, the light bands are sulfide ore minerals. The sample is from the Kimberley deposit, British Columbia. (Millimeter scale.)

the once-molten mass becomes a lens of pyrrhotite with small grains of chalcopyrite and nickel minerals scattered throughout.

Deposits formed by this process are important mostly as a source of nickel, but copper is always produced as a by-product. Examples are the deposits at Sudbury, Ontario, Thompson Lake, Manitoba, and Kambalda, Western Australia. The future may bring a different role for such deposits, however, because huge potential resources of copper ores formed by magmatic segregation have been found to lie within the Duluth Gabbro, a large igneous complex in Minnesota.

6. *Other kinds of deposits.* A few deposits cannot be classified as members of the five groups just discussed. One, a stratabound deposit but with many differences from the types above, is called red-bed copper because it is always found in red-colored sedimentary rocks. Another unusual type belongs to a curious class of intrusive igneous rock called carbonatite. Though presently a class with but one example (Palabora, South Africa), it may in fact be a more common but still little-recognized type of deposit.

Finally, we must mention the remarkable nodular growths of hydrous iron and manganese oxides found at many sites on the deep-sea floor. These slow-growing masses apparently derive their manganese and iron from hydrothermal circulation systems of the kind that form massive sulfide deposits, but just how the material is transferred to sites distant from active volcanism remains in question. The nodular masses absorb certain charged ions, such as Ba^{++}, Cu^{++}, Co^{++}, and Ni^{++}, from trace amounts in seawater; in places they have been analyzed to contain copper content as high as 2 percent. So far, manganese nodules have been recovered only on an experimental basis. Although these deposits have not yet been mined they constitute a large and potentially important future resource of copper.

Grades and Tonnages of Identified Ores

An ore is a mass of rock that is large enough and rich enough to be mined and processed. The principal characteristics we use to describe an ore deposit are its grade and tonnage. Grade denotes the content by weight of a designated metal in an ore. For example, rock is given a grade of 2 percent copper if it contains copper equal to 2 percent of the mass of rock.

The total mass of rock in an orebody is called the tonnage. Grades may have been determined for several different portions of a well-sampled orebody, but in general all that is reported is an average grade for the total tonnage in the orebody. It is not common practice in the mining industry to disclose the variability of the grade around the average, except that a lower, or cut-off, grade is sometimes identified. Grades below the cut-off grade are too lean to be mined profitably, and tonnages of such materials are commonly excluded from reported averages. Tonnages and average grades are likely to be best known when grades are high and sampling has been intense; they are less certain for grades that fall below the cut-off, because sampling of such material will usually be sparse.

We derived the grade and tonnage numbers in our study primarily from industrial sources. The numbers, therefore, refer to tonnages of ore estimated to have an average metal content of some economic value, as determined by the sampling and statistical techniques now used in the mining industry.

Grade and Tonnage Distributions

The COMRATE report of 1975 demonstrated that copper grades within a given class of deposit exhibit a continuous distribution positively skewed to higher concentrations and that the distribution can be closely approximated by a lognormal distribution (Fig. 2.8). That is, for a given set of deposits containing known grades and tonnages of copper, a normal distribution is obtained when we plot the logarithm of the tonnages at each grade against the logarithm of the grades (Fig. 2.9). Studies by Singer et al. (1975), Agterberg and Divi (1978), and Agterberg (1980) have extended the COM-RATE report and demonstrated that lognormal distributions closely describe the distribution of grades in specific classes of deposits in defined geographic areas. We have relied on these relationships in our study by assuming that untested classes of deposits—for example, magmatic segregation deposits—also have lognormal distributions of grade, and that the distribution determined for a given class of deposit in one geographic area is the same as the distribution in another area. In addition, we have assumed that the large body of data available for massive sulfide deposits in Canada can be used to predict the tonnage and grade of undiscovered massive sulfide deposits in similar but still untested rocks in the United States.

We calculated the mean of the logarithms of the tonnages of ore and the mean of the logarithm of the grades for all deposits sampled. The two means, plus their variances, automatically define the shape of the lognormal distribution curves. We then used the curves to predict grade and tonnage distributions of undiscovered ore deposits.

Each chemical element is present to some degree in each kind of rock in the earth's crust. A classic study by Ahrens (1954) demonstrated that the logarithm of the grade of a common chemical element in different rock types and the logarithm of the tonnage of the different kinds of rocks display normal distributions. Ahrens's studies were restricted to geochemically abundant elements, those that have average concentrations in the earth's crust of 0.1 percent or more by weight. Whether the grades and tonnages of trace elements in the crust (those with average concentrations in the crust below 0.1 percent by weight) also have lognormal distributions is unknown. By presuming that trace elements do have lognormal distributions, Brink (1971) derived a relationship to predict the grade and tonnage of undiscovered copper deposits in the crust. Brink assumed that copper deposits form the high-grade end of a lognormal distribution of all the copper in the crust, as shown in Figure 2.9. He presumed that all the individual lognormal distributions for each rock type, for each class of deposit, and for all geologic environments must, when calculated, yield an overall lognormal distribution. The idea has never been adequately tested, but if it is correct, all one needs to know are the means and variances for the distribution of copper in the crust as a whole and one can immediately

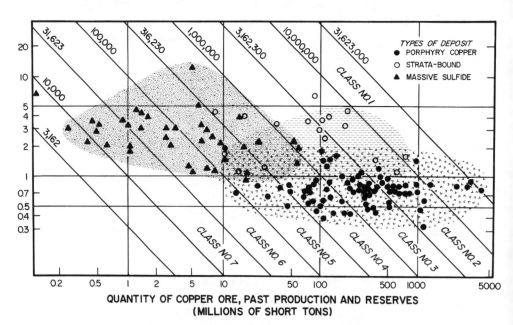

Figure 2.8 Distribution by grade and tonnage of three major classes of copper deposits. The diagonal lines show the tons of copper metal contained per deposit. Classes refer to distribution of world copper deposits by metal contained. (After COMRATE 1975.)

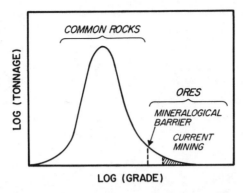

Figure 2.9   Lognormal distribution of copper in the crust. The area represented by current mining is shaded and the position of the mineralogical barrier indicated.

calculate the amount of rock that is ore under any given set of economic and technical conditions.

The assumption of a single lognormal distribution for all trace elements in the crust as a whole has been questioned. Skinner (1976) argued that even though grade and tonnage of a trace element may have lognormal distributions in common rocks, there seems to be a different lognormal distribution for that same element in ore deposits. The basis of the argument is that the special combinations of events needed to form ore deposits might just as reasonably produce a bimodal distribution in the crust—one for common rocks, another for ore deposits—in which each mode has a lognormal distribution (Fig. 2.10). Skinner's suggestion has been examined

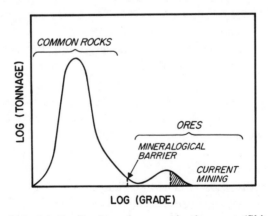

Figure 2.10   A bimodal distribution of copper in the crust (Skinner 1976). The assumption that each mode is lognormal is supported by the work of Cox (1979).

by Deffeyes and MacGregor (1978) for uranium and found to be unlikely, and by Cox (1979), for copper and found to be probable. In no case, however, has the suggestion of a bimodal distribution yet been proven or even adequately tested. Because of the uncertainty surrounding the overall distribution of copper in the crust, we have not employed the Brink method—or similar methods—to estimate the amount of copper that can be recovered. We have, instead, prepared an inventory in terms of geologic province and types of deposit to be expected.

Mining Copper Ores

Mining methods have changed greatly in scale but little in principle over the last two thousand years. The earliest methods, once surface deposits were exhausted, involved digging a small shaft or tunnel through which the ore could be selectively extracted. Underground mining methods today are designed to do the same. Selectivity is an advantage of underground mining; only the rich ore need be extracted while waste rock or uneconomically low-grade ore is left underground. Disadvantages include the large amounts of energy required to ventilate the mine, pump water out, and haul the ore in small quantities through narrow mine openings; the large-scale use of explosives to break the rock; and the need for a skilled labor force. Kellogg (1977) has estimated the gross energy requirements for mining a metric ton of rock by underground means at 130 to 400 megajoules.

Surface or open-pit methods require less energy. Open-pit mines are large, roughly conical pits (Fig. 2.11) from which underlying ore is dug out and the overlying waste rock (called overburden) discarded. The method requires the removal of one-and-a-half to four times more waste rock than ore, and because mining operations tend to be very large, selective mining is not so effective in open pits as it is underground. But ventilation is not needed, dewatering the mine is relatively easy, haulage can be carried out in huge trucks, and large-scale, low-cost blasting is effective. Economies of scale and the advantages of working in the open air offset the cost of overburden removal. Kellogg's estimates of energy demands for open-pit mining are 30–50 megajoules per metric ton.

Most copper produced today comes from ore mined by the open-pit method. As blasting has become more efficient and haulage trucks larger, the grade of ore that can be mined economically, even with high overburden-to-ore ratios, has declined steadily by more than a factor of four over the last one hundred years (Fig. 2.12). Modern copper mining offers an

Figure 2.11 Toquepala mine, Peru, a large porphyry copper deposit being exploited by open-pit mining. This photograph was taken in the 1960s, but pits today follow an identical mining practice. Rich ore is exposed on the lower three benches; both ore and overburden are contained in the upper levels, the amount of ore decreasing upward. As mining continues in an open pit and deeper benches are opened, the width of the pit is increased by moving the benches back. As a result, the ratio of ore to overburden removed decreases with time. (Courtesy of ASARCO Inc.)

excellent example of the way technological efficiencies can lower the grade of ore that can be worked economically. However, evidence suggests that a limit to the decline in minable grade may have been reached. The grade-versus-time curve (Fig. 2.12) has not only flattened; it now shows signs of rising.

The only mining technique that might be called new, in the sense that it is a product of modern technology, is solution mining, or "in situ leaching." So far this method has proved to be of very minor importance. In solution mining the ore body is fractured in place by explosives set off in a series of

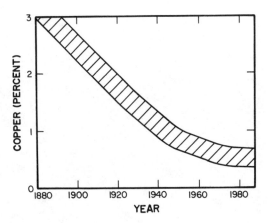

Figure 2.12　Declining minimum grade of copper ore mined economically in the United States. (After U.S. Bureau of Mines.)

tunnels or drill holes prepared for the purpose. A solvent is then percolated through the broken mass to dissolve and remove the valuable minerals. This method has yielded limited success in some copper deposits and much greater success in uranium deposits. Its drawback is that it consumes expensive solvent reagents, which are lost by reaction with valueless minerals. When and if that problem is solved, in situ leaching may prove a potent addition to the arsenal of techniques available to a mining engineer. At present it is an area for potential technological advances.

For the purposes of the model calculations, we have assumed that over the time period in question all copper will be extracted by either underground or open-pit mining operations. Costs arising from mining operations were computed from the studies of O'Hara (1980). Because many of the assumed deposits are still to be found, we added a discovery charge that is proportional to the depth and inversely proportional to the size of the deposit.

Milling and Smelting Copper Ores

After copper ore has been mined, it is processed by milling, smelting, and refining to make copper metal. Milling involves two steps—comminution, or crushing the ore, and beneficiation, or physical separation of the copper minerals from as much of the gangue as possible, by processes such as froth flotation. The beneficiated ore is then smelted to reduce the copper minerals to metal and remove the remaining gangue. Most copper smelting today utilizes pyrometallurgy (processes carried out in furnaces at high temperature), but some copper is produced by hydrometallurgy, in which the copper is leached out of crushed ore with chemical solvents and recovered from the leach solutions by electrolysis or chemical methods. Hydrometallurgical processes now account for only about 15 percent of copper production (Biswas and Davenport 1980:254) and are not expected to displace pyrometallurgy in the near future because of their high energy costs. After smelting, copper is refined to bring it to the high standard of purity required for today's applications.

Copper is not the easiest metal to extract from its ore, but it was the first to be smelted in both the Old World and the New. The early smelters of copper used ores containing nonsulfide minerals (called oxide ores). The ore was broken into small pieces and beneficiated by hand. Because considerable gangue remained in it, the smelting process had to accomplish two objectives: reduction of the ore minerals to metal and removal of the gangue. The reduction process was accomplished by heating the ore in the presence of carbon monoxide gas, formed by the combustion of charcoal. Gangue was removed by mixing the ore with a flux that reacted with the worthless silicate minerals to form a slag. The temperature required for smelting depended on the melting point of the slag rather than the requirements of ore reduction. In the case of an iron-oxide (or iron-ore) flux, the temperature required was 1,200°C, which could be attained in a simple charcoal-fired bowl furnace blown with a bellows. Liquid slag and molten copper are immiscible; the slag, being less dense, floated on top of the copper, which was tapped from the furnace into an ingot mold.

Deposits of oxide ores are scarce, and most of those in the Old World were exhausted early in the Bronze Age, by 3000 B.C. In their absence early metallurgists turned to sulfide ores such as chalcopyrite ($CuFeS_2$), which contain iron as well as copper. The basic problem in the pyrometallurgy of the sulfide ores of copper is to separate the metal from the gangue and the iron from the copper with a minimal amount of fuel. There are two ways of going about this. One is to convert the sulfide minerals to oxides by mixing the ore with burning charcoal in open heaps, a process known as dead roasting, and then to smelt as before. The other is to melt the sulfide minerals and effect a separation of the gangue and part of the iron as a slag while the copper is retained in the molten sulfide, called matte. The matte is then converted to metal.

Matte smelting requires less fuel than dead roasting and reduction of the resulting oxides; by medieval times it was the established method of copper smelting. It still required much fuel, however. In the sixteenth century 20 tons of fuel were required to smelt one ton of copper (an energy consumption of about 500 megajoules/kilogram), and this ratio had not changed much by the mid-nineteenth century (Tylecote 1976:94). Consequently, during the early industrial period copper smelters were located where fuel was abundant, as in South Wales. In the late nineteenth and early twentieth centuries the principal developments in copper smelting were the adoption of a form of Bessemer converter for making metal from matte, beneficiation of ores by flotation, electrolytic refining for attaining the high degree of purity required for electrical applications, and a substantial reduction in energy consumption.

Milling Copper Ore

Ore must be ground finely enough to liberate the copper minerals from the unwanted gangue minerals in which they are dispersed. This requires breaking the rock matrix (as shown in Fig. 2.4) away from individual mineral grains. Because copper ore is low grade, much rock must be broken to liberate a small amount of ore mineral.

Two physical processes effect comminution: the splitting of rock particles by brittle fracture (the dominant process in crushing) and the removal of fine particles from large pieces of rock by abrasion (the dominant process in grinding). Crushing fractures individual chunks of rock by direct application of force, and the energy required, the fracture energy, is listed for representative types of rock in Table 2.2. Note that the rock proposed as the ore most likely to be used if ever we reach the point where common rock must supply copper—which we call the backstop ore—is basalt, one of the most difficult rocks to crush. Rock crushing is relatively inefficient; only about 10 percent of the power supplied to the crusher goes to form the new surface area, the rest being dissipated as heat (Harris 1966).

Crushing is impractical once the rock has been reduced to a size of about 20–50 millimeters, because the individual pieces of rock cannot be maneuvered into contact with the crushing jaws. Further size reduction must be effected by grinding, in which rock particles are abraded by means of rubbing contact with each other and with metal balls or rods. The energy efficiency of ore grinding is extremely low. Approximately 50 percent of all the energy used in ore beneficiation in the United States is consumed in grinding, with more than 97 percent of this dissipated as heat (Hartley,

Prisbrey, and Wick 1978). The optimal particle size is the size at which recovery of copper minerals during subsequent flotation is maximized; for typical copper ores this is in the range of 10 to 50 millimeters in diameter. Finer grinding will not be required for the backstop ore, but the quantity of rock that must be processed for the same copper output will be about two orders of magnitude greater than that needed for the lowest-grade sulfide ores today.

Beneficiation is the mechanical separation of ore-mineral particles from silicate-mineral particles produced by grinding. The degree to which ore is separated from gangue sets an upper bound to the degree of beneficiation that can be obtained; ideally, all gangue particles should be separated from all particles of ore minerals. Figure 2.13 suggests why complete separation cannot be achieved in grinding: for ore to be detached completely from gangue, grinding to a particle size much smaller than the grain size of the ore minerals is required. For copper ores this amount of grinding would produce dust-size particles too small for effective beneficiation.

Beneficiation processes make use of differences in the physical properties of ore and gangue minerals. Gravity separation, for example, is used when the denser ore minerals can be made to settle more rapidly from a liquid than can the less dense gangue. In froth flotation, the most effective method of beneficiating copper ores, the pulverized ore is agitated in water

Table 2.2 Fracture energies of representative types of rock

Rock	Fracture energy[a] (J/m^2)
Basalt	200
Granite	200
Quartzite	177
Marble	128
Sandstone	87
Limestone	52

Source: Peck, Nolen-Hoeksema, Barton, and Gordon. 1985.

a. Fracture energy is the energy required per unit area to create new surface, in joules per square meter.

Table 2.3 Energy consumption in milling copper ore

Milling operation	Energy used (kJ/kg)
Crushing	8
Grinding	40
Flotation	9
Total	57

Source: Joe 1979.

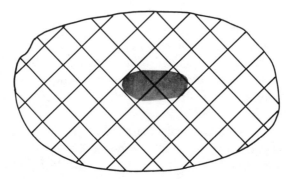

Figure 2.13   Sketch representing a piece of rock containing a grain of ore mineral (shaded). When the rock is ground to a particle size comparable to the size of the ore mineral grain, as suggested by the area of the intersecting lines, the ore mineral remains attached to the rock; grinding to much finer size is required to effect separation of the ore from the gangue. For most copper ores, grinding to this degree would produce dust-size particles.

containing a reagent (called a collector), which is adsorbed on the surface of the mineral grains, and a frother, which facilitates bubble formation. Sulfide minerals are separated from gangue by a collector that makes the bubbles attach to them; if the sulfide particles are small enough, the attached bubbles will carry them into a froth that forms at the top of the flotation cell, from which it is collected (Wills 1981:376). The froth is then dewatered. Copper ore that contains 0.5 percent copper can be beneficiated to 30 percent copper by flotation (Biswas and Davenport 1980:59).

The amount of energy consumed in milling copper ore appears in Table 2.3. Milling produces large amounts of waste, called tailings, which in the past were usually dumped in the nearest river or stream. Now they are often impounded behind dams in ponds, but storage of this kind can be a source of environmental problems such as contamination of groundwater or release of toxic dust. Disposal of tailings has been only 5 percent of the cost of milling copper ores in the past (Biswas and Davenport 1980:395), but this will not be the case in the future as the volume of tailings increases and as tolerance decreases for the resulting environmental degradation.

Smelting Copper Ore

The concentrates produced by milling can be roasted, but modern practice is to place the concentrate directly into a large reverberatory furnace for the first step in the matte smelting. The furnace can be fired with oil, gas, or powdered coal. When the charge is melted, slag forms from the gangue minerals still present in the concentrate and from the iron in the ore minerals. This slag floats on top of the liquid copper-iron sulfide matte and can be tapped off. In modern smelters, heat released by the partial oxidation of the sulfides in the charge is used to reduce the consumption of fuel. If oxygen rather than air is used in the furnace, essentially no fuel is required (Queneau 1981).

The liquid matte is tapped from the reverberatory furnace and transferred to a converter, a vessel similar to the Bessemer converter formerly used in steelmaking, where air or oxygen is blown over it. The iron sulfide remaining in the matte oxidizes first and is removed from the converter as slag. With continued blowing, part of the copper sulfide oxidizes and reacts with the remaining copper sulfide to form liquid copper metal and sulfur dioxide gas.

Two separate steps are taken to refine the crude copper made in the converter. In fire refining, impurities in the copper are oxidized and removed as slag. The copper is deoxidized with hydrocarbons (such as natural gas) and cast into plates known as anodes. Electrolytic refining of the anodes accomplishes the final purification.

Efficiency and Costs

The recovery of copper in modern pyrometallurgical smelting is very high. Of the copper that enters the smelter, about 0.5 percent is lost as dust in the stack gases and 1–2 percent in the slags (Biswas and Davenport 1980:214). As treatment of stack gases to reduce sulfur emissions increases in prevalence and efficiency, more of the copper-containing dust can be recovered. The slag can be crushed and beneficiated as if it were ore, but little room remains for improved recovery of copper in smelting practice. Recovery of metal during beneficiation is only about 80 percent, however (Chapman and Roberts 1983:111), and improved technology may reduce losses of copper in the tailings produced in milling.

Production of copper requires almost twice as much energy per unit weight of metal produced as does iron production (Chapman and Roberts 1983:114), owing to the low grade of copper ores, which even after beneficiation are much leaner than iron ores. But copper is easier to reduce than iron. The thermodynamic efficiency, the fraction of the energy used in smelting that goes into breaking chemical bonds to release metal from the ore minerals, is eighteen times smaller for copper than for iron because of the large amount of waste rock and iron sulfide in the concentrate that has to be heated along with the copper-containing minerals.

The traditional concern of copper smelters, to reduce fuel requirements, will continue to be of interest in the future. Hydrometallurgical processes are even less energy efficient than pyrometallurgy, with the further disadvantage that electrowinning requires electrical energy, the most expensive use of energy (Kellogg 1977). (The cost of electrolytic refining of copper is small compared with the cost of electrowinning copper from leaching solutions.) We expect the thermodynamic efficiency of pyrometallurgy to decrease somewhat as ore grades decline, unless some new method of beneficiation is discovered. When it becomes necessary to extract copper from silicate rock, the energy required for smelting will increase by more than an order of magnitude, because the volume of material that must be heated will be greater and the chemical bonds that must be broken will be stronger. We expect that copper smelters will have to face new technological problems in the disposal of wastes and in securing adequate supplies of water as lower-grade ores are used. At present, 648 tons of solid waste are left for disposal for each ton of copper produced (Chapman and Roberts 1983:19). As long as smelters exist in areas of low population density, the wastes can be left in piles above ground or in tailings ponds. Only about half this waste is suitable for back-filling mine openings (Wills 1981:472).

Sulfur emissions from copper smelting have been a source of environmental degradation for a long time. The copper smelters in South Wales were described thus in 1813: "In the neighborhood of Wansla there are some very extensive copper works, which are situated in a hollow and immediately above them is not a blade of grass, a green bush, nor any form of vegetation, while volumes of smoke, thick and pestilential, are crawling up the sides of the hills, which are as bare as a turnpike road" (quoted in Trinder 1982:100). Smelter waste gases can be used to make sulfuric acid, but in the United States, where sulfur is abundant and cheap, this has not been economic. Consequently, sulfur is removed from stack gases only in response to environmental regulations, but there will be no sulfur emission problem once copper ore has been exhausted and the metal is extracted from silicate rock.

The amount of water used in milling copper ore is now about 850 gallons per ton (Chapman and Roberts 1983:111). We expect this to increase as ores become leaner. Many copper mines and mills are in arid regions, such as northern Chile and Arizona; the provision of an adequate supply of copper in the face of competing demands for water may become difficult as very low grade ores are milled. The much larger quantities of water that will be required for milling backstop ore will be an even more serious problem.

Copper Resources of the United States

We include in our model copper resources of the forty-eight continental states of the United States; Alaska, Hawaii, and Puerto Rico are excluded. This sampling introduces an element of artificiality because both Alaska and Puerto Rico are known to have copper resources and both have production records. Present production of copper in these areas is small, however, and we do not believe that their exclusion dramatically influences our final conclusions. A more serious problem arises from the exclusion of at least one potential resource—manganiferous nodules on the deep-sea floor—located at the boundaries of the region under study. Similar limitations would apply if any other large area of the globe were selected for study. Short of considering the entire globe, therefore, we cannot avoid this problem. As we shall explain when sensitivity tests of our model calculations are discussed in Chapter 5, the possible errors introduced by resource exclusions do not change our conclusions; they merely change the dates at which some of the predicted shifts in use patterns will occur.

To assess the undiscovered copper resources of the United States, we divided the country into seven geologic provinces on the basis of the dominant class of copper deposit known or believed to occur in each area. For each province we calculated distribution functions for grades and tonnages of deposits and for depth of deposits, using as a basis either the geology of the province or, if insufficient data existed, the geology of better-known provinces of similar character elsewhere in the world.

For illustrative purposes, we summarize below our techniques for estimating resources in two of the seven geologic provinces, the massive sulfide deposits of the Precambrian basement in the eastern half of the country and the stratabound deposits, late Precambrian in age, in a group of sedimentary rocks called the Belt Supergroup found in Montana and Idaho.

The Precambrian Basement, Eastern United States

Ancient metamorphic rocks of the Precambrian age are exposed in much of Canada east of the Rockies, comprising a geologic province known as the

Canadian Shield. The region is richly mineralized and was for a long time the mainstay of Canada's mining industry. Much of the United States is also underlain by rocks of Precambrian vintage that are actually a continuation of the Canadian Shield. In the United States, however, most of the Precambrian basement is overlain by thousands of feet of younger sedimentary rocks, which are unlikely to contain substantial copper deposits. Where the Precambrian basement does crop out in the United States, as in Wisconsin and Minnesota, we find deposits similar to those in Canada. We have every reason to expect, therefore, that the buried Precambrian basement in the United States contains the same kinds of deposits as in Canada. We presumed for purposes of our study that mining could be carried down to 15,000 feet—deeper than any mines today but the depth to which planning and development is now being directed in the world's deepest mines, the gold mines of the Witwatersrand Basin in South Africa. We assumed, therefore, that eventually copper mining will be carried to these depths too, but we recognize that the assumption is optimistic—the South African mines are favored by a very gentle thermal gradient, whereas the United States has either a normal or, in places, a steep gradient. A 15,000-foot mine in the United States will be much hotter than a gold mine of the same depth in South Africa.

To model the availability of copper from the Precambrian basement of the United States, we assumed that equal volumes of Precambrian basement rocks in Canada and the United States that share similar geologic histories will contain the same number of mineral deposits. Most of the Canadian deposits are massive sulfide deposits encased in volcanic rocks, and we have assumed such will also be the case for the United States. Our data base for Canadian massive sulfide deposits came, through the courtesy of Donald Sangster (personal communication, 1980), from the working files of the Geological Survey of Canada, wherein is compiled a list of grades and tonnages of all massive sulfide deposits known to occur in the Canadian Shield.

The shield is far from homogeneous. Different regions experienced distinctly different geologic histories and exhibit different degrees of mineralization. To account for heterogeneity we divided the Canadian Shield into four regions with different tectonic histories: the Superior, Grenville, and Keweenawan, plus the combined Churchill and Nain provinces (combined because they are of similar ages; Goldich et al. 1966). We ignored the Grenville region because it is comparatively sparse in copper deposits. The remaining regions contain copper deposits and correspond to similar regions in the United States that are known from deep drilling to lie beneath the sedimentary cover (Goldich et al. 1966). There are also a few small regions of the Precambrian basement in the United States that do not correspond exactly to the major tectonic regions in the exposed Canadian Shield. For our study the unique regions of the United States either were added to the regions closest in age—the Elsonian terrain was added to the Black Hills, and the Llano Uplift to the U.S. Grenville province (Goldich et al. 1966)—or they were ignored because they do not contain significant copper resources in those areas of the United States in which they do appear at the surface. We are confident that such minor assumptions do not significantly influence our results.

For each geologic region of the Canadian Shield we calculated distributions of grades and tonnages of the known deposits. Next we measured the area of each tectonic region in Canada and the United States by planimetry of the *Tectonic Map of North America* (King 1969) and figure 6 of Goldich et al. (1966). We presumed the distributions were identical in the tested and untested provinces. To estimate a distribution of deposit by depth, we assumed that the sedimentary rock cover above the basement is barren and that the distribution of deposits within the basement rocks is uniform down to a total depth of 15,000 feet.

We arrived at the distribution of deposits by depth in the following manner. Exploration for massive sulfide deposits depends heavily on geophysical methods of detection, and with present technology it is possible to find deposits that reach only within 1,000 feet of the surface (Charles River Associates 1978). We therefore assumed that Sangster's data are exhaustive to a depth of 3,000 feet (we allowed 2,000 feet for the height of the orebody) but described none of the deposits that might occur at greater depths. This assumption is likely to be a pessimistic estimate of near-surface resources in the shield because more deposits will surely be found in Canada but, owing to the difficulties of exploring for deposits through thousands of feet of sedimentary cover rocks, the assumption is optimistic for the United States. We feel our estimate of the resource base is probably on the low side.

The Belt Supergroup, Montana

The Belt Supergroup is a widespread unit of sedimentary rocks within which some strata of the Revett Formation contain extensive stratabound copper deposits. Cox et al. (1973) assessed the subeconomic resources of stratabound copper deposits in the western United States at 20 million tons of copper. Their estimate included other sedimentary copper deposits besides those found in the Belt Supergroup—deposits such as Nacimiento and Creta, red-bed coppers that are small and have different geologies from those in the Belt. Because resources of the Belt dominate the sedimentary deposits of the West, however, we neglected the other deposits and presumed that 20 million tons is a realistic estimate of copper in the stratabound deposits of the Belt.

We assumed, perhaps optimistically, that the grades and tonnages of the Belt deposits have distributions like the geologically similar stratabound deposits in Zambia: the Zambian and the Belt deposits are of late-Proterozoic age and both are found in sedimentary rocks. The Zambian deposits are considerably higher in grade than the Belt deposits are likely to be, with a mean arithmetic grade of 3.78 percent copper (Singer et al. 1975), whereas those of the Belt are 1 percent or less (Brobst and Pratt 1973). But our estimation procedure requires that we know the variances of grade and tonnage of the deposits in addition to the means, so rather than inventing variances we depended on the only study of stratabound deposit grades and tonnages extant—that of Singer et al. (1975) for the Zambian deposits.

Finally, to estimate depths of rock overlying the Belt Supergroup deposits, we constructed a simplified geologic model of the Libby Quadrangle in Northwest Montana, which covers almost half the area in which significant copper deposits are known to occur (Clark 1971). We assumed that model depths in the Libby Quadrangle are applicable to the Belt Supergroup as a whole. Further, we assumed all the mineral deposits in the Belt are uniformly distributed through a single stratum, the top of the Revett Formation (Harrison 1972).

Estimation of a Supply Function for Copper

In that the distributions of deposits in the different classes by size and grade were taken from the literature, our study does not provide new information on this point. Our calculation of distributions of deposits by depth and the total copper resources available in each of the seven geologic provinces does include new material, as shown in Table 2.4.

The major innovation in our study is the conversion of such data into a cost function—that is, a relation between costs and geologic variables of grade, tonnage, and depth. First, as previously mentioned, we added a cost of discovery that increases with deposit depth and is inversely proportional to the deposit size. We then estimated the cost of producing copper from the ground by using the empirical cost curves developed by O'Hara (1980) from the data on open-pit and underground mining operations in the United

Table 2.4 Magnitude and depth distribution of copper resources in sulfide deposits in the United States

Province and deposit type	Total copper resource (short tons copper)	Depth distribution (to top of orebody)
Duluth Complex, Minnesota (magmatic segregate)	126×10^6	48% to 3,000 ft 35% to 9,000 ft 17% to 14,000 ft
Precambrian basement, eastern United States 　Superior province	5.4×10^6	34.8% to 3,000 ft 38.2% to 9,000 ft 26.9% to 14,000 ft
Black Hills and Elsonian	14.5×10^6	19.8% to 3,000 ft 44.8% to 9,000 ft 35.3% to 14,000 ft
Keweenawan (mainly massive sulfide)	13.4×10^6	10.5% to 5,000 ft 80.8% to 9,000 ft 8.7% to 14,000 ft
Belt Supergroup, Montana (stratabound)	20×10^6	30.4% to 3,000 ft 28.6% to 9,000 ft 41.0% to 14,000 ft
White Pine Area, Michigan (mainly stratabound)	16×10^6	40% to 3,000 ft 40% to 9,000 ft 20% to 14,000 ft
Appalachians (mainly porphyry)	11×10^6	20% to 1,640 ft 20% to 4,950 ft 20% to 8,200 ft 20% to 11,480 ft 20% to 14,760 ft
Southwest United States (mainly porphyry)	159×10^6	50% to 1,640 ft 50% to 4,920 ft
Basin and range in Utah and Nevada	125×10^6	67.1% to 3,000 ft 22.2% to 9,000 ft 10.7% to 14,000 ft
Total	490.3×10^6	

States and Canada. Certain extrapolations were needed, such as that which projects experience in underground mining, currently extending to depths of about 5,000 feet in the United States and Canada, down to depths of 15,000 feet. We also found that in order to make the data accumulated in our study compatible with O'Hara's curves, we had to introduce the following assumptions:

1. In open-pit mines, the orebody was assumed to be a sphere and the open-pit mine to be a conical excavation with sides 25° from horizontal, except for the Duluth Complex, where the great strength of the surrounding rock would permit the development of pits with walls at 45° (INCO 1975).
2. Mines were assumed to operate for 20 years, with depreciation following a straight-line formula.
3. Mines and mills were assumed to operate for three shifts a day, seven days a week, with 10 percent downtime for maintenance and strikes.
4. Refining and transportation costs were assumed to be constant over time, at $0.55 per kilogram of copper metal.

The model determined automatically whether underground or surface mining was cheaper for each deposit. When our data were fed into the model it soon became clear that larger resources of copper than are present in ore deposits would eventually have to be mined. Therefore, we added two additional low-grade sources of copper, as follows.

Copper in Very Low Grade Sulfide Deposits

As we discussed, to form separate ore minerals copper must attain a minimum grade in a rock; below a grade of about 0.1 percent, copper will be dissolved in common silicate minerals. The published data that we used in our estimating procedure were usually discontinued at a grade of 0.4 percent, because very little is known about deposits that are subeconomic by today's standards.

To account for these copper deposits with grades between 0.4 percent and the mineralogical barrier of 0.1 percent, we have included the 110×10^6 short tons of copper estimated by Cox et al. (1973) to fall in this range. The material in this category includes copper in small, low-grade deposits at all depths, plus larger, low-grade deposits that are deeply buried. A few large, low-grade deposits that are known and reported, because they are near the surface, were included in our specific region estimates. Beneficiation and smelting costs for the low-grade deposits should be similar to those for large, near-surface, low-grade deposits, but mining costs will be higher. We have therefore taken a figure 20 percent higher than the most expensive of the regularly computed cost categories. The costs of producing all of the copper estimated to be present in sulfide deposits to a depth of 15,000 feet are listed in Table 2.5. The deposits have been divided into twenty-one

Table 2.5 Resource availability and production costs for copper[a]

Resource category	Production cost ($/kg)	Copper available in the category (million tons)[b]
1	1.023	3,111.000
2	1.209	11,654.900
3	1.395	20,090.000
4	1.581	2,911.500
5	1.767	27,427.700
6	2.046	15,546.000
7	2.232	36,479.500
8	2.418	17,795.300
9	2.604	12,616.400
10	2.790	40,597.300
11	3.069	38,774.300
12	3.441	49,404.300
13	3.813	37,459.100
14	4.185	23,092.200
15	4.557	14,693.400
16	5.115	25,432.300
17	5.859	18,829.300
18	6.603	17,813.500
19	7.719	13,378.300
20	11.160	16,706.900
21	13.950	90,700.000
22	102.300	—

a. All costs are given in 1978 U.S. dollars. The supply curve is approximated by appropriate stepwise linear functions, and production costs include all processing costs from ore to metal and are the average costs in each category.

b. A ton is equal to 1,000 kilograms, or 1.1 short tons.

categories on the basis of the per-kilogram cost of producing copper from the deposits; the twenty-second category is the infinitely large backstop resource.

Backstop Resources

It is possible (or indeed likely, if our model estimates are correct) that the entire supply of copper ores above the mineralogical barrier of 0.1 percent will be exhausted sometime in the next two centuries. What will happen at that point? Will our economy go without copper? Will a substitute be used? Or will we turn to very low grade ore found at very low concentrations (and presumably very high cost) in common rock?

In order to hazard an answer to these questions, we must first understand the production of copper from superabundant but high-cost sources, which we have identified as backstop copper. A backstop resource is one that is available in essentially unlimited quantities—for example, energy produced from fusion, fresh water derived from seawater, and optical fibers made from common sand. Once an economy begins relying on a backstop resource, that resource is no longer scarce; it cannot be depleted.

When deposits of grade 0.1 percent or higher are exhausted, copper will have to be recovered from common rocks, where it occurs in solid solution in silicate minerals. Copper is not uniformly distributed but is more likely to be found in certain minerals, such as biotite, pyroxene, and amphibole. Beneficiation is possible only to the extent that these minerals can be concentrated. Consider the case of a rock containing 0.02 percent copper, all of which is in pyroxene ($FeSiO_3$), where the pyroxene makes up 30 percent by weight of the rock. The richest concentrate possible is only 0.067 percent. The copper must be recovered by breaking down the host silicate mineral, in much the same way as it has been proposed to recover aluminum from silicate minerals when bauxite ores are finally mined out.

The common-rock types with the highest copper contents are the mafic igneous rocks such as basalt and gabbro and the intermediate igneous rocks such as diorite. The average content of copper in all rocks of the continental crust is about 0.007 percent, but a few mafic igneous rocks have been found to have levels of 0.05 percent copper. If we accept that 10 percent of all mafic rocks have copper contents of 0.05 percent and that 20 percent of the volume of the crust to a depth of 1.5 kilometers consists of mafic igneous rocks or their metamorphic derivatives, we can calculate that the United States contains about 3.5×10^{11} tons of potentially recoverable copper in the uppermost 1.5 kilometers of the crust. This is the figure we use for the quantity of backstop copper in our model.

Estimating the cost of production of such copper is difficult in the extreme, with the energy requirement being the only relatively solid figure we can identify. The energy needed to recover copper locked in solid solution in silicate minerals is much greater than the energy needed to recover copper from sulfide ores of the same grade. The differences, which have been estimated by Skinner (1979), depend somewhat on grade, because mining costs per ton of rock are the same for the two ores but concentrating and processing costs rise more steeply as grades of silicate ores decline than they do for sulfide ores. The difference in the amount of energy needed to work a 0.05 percent sulfide ore, if one existed, and a 0.05 percent silicate ore is estimated to be a factor of ten (Skinner 1979).

No estimates exist of the total costs of producing backstop copper. A rough guess is that total costs will rise only by a factor of five as we move from sulfide ores to common rock. Following the cost argument for working sulfide ores below grades of 0.4 percent copper, we estimate a large body of 0.05 percent sulfide ore could probably be worked for about $22 per kilogram of recovered copper. This means that a large body of silicate ore at a grade of 0.05 percent might be mined and processed for $110 per kilogram of copper.

Any facility that produced copper from ordinary rock would probably have to process a million or more tons of rock a day. Production costs should therefore include any additional and special costs associated with processing huge volumes of rock, such as the costs of storing and processing the wastes, treating vast quantities of water, and reclaiming the land after mining. Because of the scale involved there is no directly applicable experience from which we can make an estimate of such environmental costs, but assuming complex restoration problems and severe water contamination difficulties, costs might run as high as $5 per ton of mined ore, or about $11 per kilogram of recovered copper. The full cost of recovering copper from the richest silicate sources is therefore estimated to be about $121 per kilogram.

Consequences of Mining the Predicted Copper Resources

We assume in our model not only that all copper deposits to a depth of 15,000 feet will be discovered but also that backstop copper will be produced from common rocks. Of necessity we have limited the model to quantifiable technical questions. But what of societal and environmental questions? Copper extraction in the United States and the world has risen, albeit erratically, for the last century (Fig. 2.14). Our model predicts the rise will continue. Maximum production rates during the years we mine sulfide ores of even the lowest grades are about 9×10^9 kilograms of copper a year, a rate that will be reached some fifty years hence. By comparison, rates of about 2×10^9 kilograms per year will pertain in the immediate future. A copper mining industry 4.5 times larger than today's will probably not cause environmental problems too difficult to manage. A much greater problem is that some of the stratiform ore in the Belt Supergroup lies in Glacier National Park, and a sizable fraction of the ore in the Duluth Gabbro is in or immediately adjacent to the Boundary Waters region in Minnesota. Whether society would ever allow these beautiful spots to be disturbed by mining is very doubtful. If we cannot mine them, the advent of backstop ores moves nearer.

When we consider mining backstop ores we are confronted with different environmental problems. Although they may be technically solvable—indeed our model presumes they are and assigns a cost for the solutions—we have to wonder whether society at large will accept the consequences.

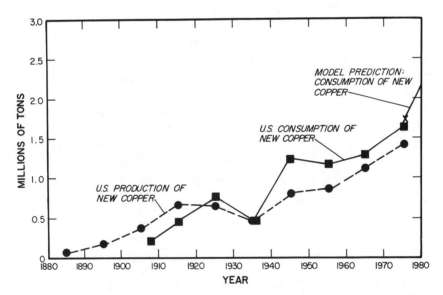

Figure 2.14 Consumption and production of copper in the United States. (After U.S. Bureau of Mines, and *World Mining,* Annual Review, 1985.)

We suggest that during a decade in the late twenty-first century the United States will produce about 15×10^9 kilograms of new copper annually from backstop silicate ores. The grade of the ore is assumed to be 0.05 percent, and if recovery is 75 percent efficient, each metric ton of rock mined will yield 0.375 kilograms of copper metal. The production rate requires that 40×10^9 metric tons of rock be mined and processed each year, or 110×10^6 metric tons per day, every day of the year. Mafic igneous rock has a density of about 3 grams per cubic centimeter, which means that the volume of the rock removed and processed will have to be 13.3 cubic kilometers per year. This is so much larger than any operation today that it is hard to imagine. A huge pit operation by today's standard, such as that at Bingham Canyon, Utah, can remove about 0.4×10^6 metric tons of rock a day, whereas a Toquepala-sized operation (Fig. 2.13) can remove about 0.2×10^6 metric tons per day.

Meeting the copper needs of 2090 will therefore require 275 pit operations the size of Bingham or 550 the size of Toquepala. Even with careful planning and conservation, the processing and disposing of the waste rock will consume an enormous amount of water, about 2,000 liters per metric ton of rock mined and processed. Where will the operation obtain 2.2×10^{11} liters of clean water every day? That is 20 percent of the average discharge of the largest river in the United States, the Mississippi. Furthermore, energy demands of mining and smelting will be about 10^{10} joules per kilogram of copper produced for an overall demand of 4.1×10^{17} joules per day (3.9×10^{14} BTU per day). This is an energy use rate of 0.48×10^{13} watts. By comparison the whole world use rate of supplementary energy today is 10^{13} watts. Could one country use half that amount for copper alone?

To employ estimates of the production of copper from backstop ores, we have had to assume these problems will somehow be solved over the next century or so. From the vantage point of the middle 1980s, we cannot foresee the possible solutions; nor can we be sure that we have not overlooked a wholly different approach (such as copper-concentrating microorganisms) that will make our anxieties in retrospect appear myopic. We can today simply point to the possibility for significant economic and environmental dislocations when the time to turn to backstop ores arrives.

3 Substitution, Recycling, and Demand

All the services now performed by copper can also be obtained from one or more substitute materials. We expect that as copper becomes scarcer and its price rises, more substitutes for it will be used and more copper will be reclaimed from discarded copper-containing products. The costs of alternative sources of copper and copper services relative to the cost of new copper will determine the amount of substitution and recycling that takes place. We will investigate these costs in this chapter and close with a discussion of our method for estimating the future demand for copper.

Copper appears in a great many products today and, in principle, it would require an engineering study of the possibilities of using alternative materials in each product to determine the costs of substitution. Since case-by-case analysis of individual products would have been impractical for us to undertake, we aggregated copper-containing products into 21 demand categories, each selected so that some combination of a small number of physical properties, called the ruling properties, determined the amount of material needed to make products in that category. We then consulted engineering analyses of the substitution possibilities in each demand category to define substitution costs for the model. These same categories proved useful in projecting future demand for the services now obtained from copper. Because we were unable to find an equivalent of the ruling properties for substitution with which to establish recycling categories, we used an alternative method of aggregation based on available data in the analysis of recycling.

Substitution

A newly discovered material may be substituted in a product to obtain improved performance at lower cost[1] or an established material may be substituted owing to increased scarcity of the original constituents. Scarcity might result from exhaustion of resources, competition from other uses, or interruption of supply due to political or military actions. We can find substitutes that will give equivalent service for almost all the materials used in modern technology. Only a few metals have unique properties that make substitution for them impossible in particular applications.[2]

Use of substitute materials usually requires a higher level of technological sophistication than did the original material. Successful substitutions require both the capacity to produce the alternative material in the necessary quantities and the technological capability to redesign the product so as to use the substitute material to provide equivalent or acceptable service. There are many examples of substitutions that have become possible because of improved technology. One is the increased use of metals and minerals in the United States to provide services that were originally obtained from wood. This substitution was possible because of the development of new technological capabilities in the nineteenth-century metal-producing and metal-working industries. Many of the timber bridges and trestles originally used on railways were replaced by steel structures after 1870, when large-scale steel production in the United States was initiated (Olson 1971). The introduction of metal substitutes circumvented the constraint on economic growth that would have resulted from the eventual depletion of timber resources (see, for example, Rosenberg 1973).

Copper was the first metal to be used as an engineering material, originally in pure form and later with additions of arsenic, tin, or zinc to increase its strength (Copper Development Association 1957). Copper and its alloys are so versatile and so easily worked into useful objects that, from earliest times until well into the industrial era, they were often the materials first used in new products. Later, increased technological sophistication permitted the replacement of copper-based alloys by more specialized materials that allowed the required service to be obtained at lower cost. Iron was the first material to be used as a substitute for copper and copper alloys. When first smelted in ancient times, iron was more expensive than copper but it became cheaper as iron-making technology improved. With more experience with the metallurgy of iron came the possibility of making superior products. An axe made of iron holds a better edge than one made of bronze, and as the price of iron fell relative to that of bronze, higher-quality axes became available at lower cost.[3]

Copper has always been subject to this kind of replacement, but major new uses continued to appear until the early years of the twentieth century. The copper boilers that first provided steam for Newcomen's engines were soon replaced by iron ones, but the development of the steam engine itself created new uses for copper-based alloys—for bearing materials, condenser tubes (for stationary and marine engines), screw propellers (for steamships), and large brass nameplates (for British locomotives). Today, other materials have once again replaced copper in most of these applications. Steel roller bearings are used instead of brass journals in railway rolling stock; titanium is used for condenser tubes that would have been made of brass a few years ago; and stainless steel competes with bronze for ships' propellers. The nineteenth century brought a tremendous increase in the range of products requiring copper as its high electrical conductivity was first exploited on a large scale, but while electrical products still account for the major uses of copper today, aluminum is in direct competition with it in many of these applications.

We do not expect the expansion of the use of copper in new products, which continued through the end of the nineteenth century but diminished in the twentieth, to resume in the advanced industrial countries. Technological sophistication reduces the need for general-purpose, easily worked, but relatively expensive alloys and we foresee no other physical property of copper that is likely to warrant the exploitation its conductivity has already received. Moreover, improvements in design and manufacturing make it possible to use copper more efficiently. Thinner brass fins have replaced copper in automobile radiators; copper tubing has replaced brass pipe in plumbing; and miniaturization allows less copper to do the same work in electrical applications. Since 1965 copper consumption has been roughly constant in the United States and has been leveling off in other developed countries (NATO 1976:53). Our expectation that substitution for existing uses of copper will continue while few entirely new large-scale uses for copper will appear is the basis of our projection of the future demand for copper.

Costs

Given the technological capability to supply a substitute material and to redesign a product to use it, the use of a substitute depends on the relative costs of making and using a product with it and with the original material. Many factors contribute to the cost of using a substitute material in a given product. The easiest cost to calculate, but often the least important, is the cost of the substitute material itself. Other costs are associated with the redesign of the product and with whatever new manufacturing facilities are required, as well as with the operation of the product made with the substitute material. Suppose, for example, the copper conductors in the rotor of an electrical motor are replaced by aluminum conductors. Equipment for fabricating the aluminum conductors will be needed. Aluminum has two-thirds the conductivity of copper and about one-third the density. Hence, aluminum conductors cannot simply be inserted in place of copper ones; the motor must be redesigned. The motor will be less efficient, which means that it will run at a higher temperature (and so have a shorter service life), and it will require more electrical energy to accomplish the same amount of mechanical work.

Because it is so difficult to make reliable estimates of all the substitution costs and to establish confidence that the product made with another material will give the performance expected, manufacturers may not make or customers accept substitution even though an immediate savings can be made on the cost of materials. An example of this reluctance is the continued use of bronze and iron cannon throughout the seventeenth, eighteenth, and nineteenth centuries, although the price of iron was substantially lower than that of bronze, because the reliability of iron cannon under the varied and uncertain conditions of military or naval service was doubted. When the savings and effectiveness of a substitute material can be conclusively demonstrated, however, substitution may take place rapidly. This was the case for aluminum conductors in the long-distance transmission of high-voltage electrical power; the larger volume of the aluminum wires needed to obtain equivalent conductance is not a disadvantage for overhead lines, and the lighter weight of aluminum wire saves on the cost of support structures. These savings are easily calculated and their value quickly demonstrated in practice.

Other writers who have considered some of the substitution costs discussed above have predicted that future technological changes will facilitate substitution for scarce resources. Futurists often suggest that substitution offers salvation from the consequences of mineral resource exhaustion. They base their arguments on extrapolation of past successes and ask us to have faith in the continued growth of technological capability and abundant energy resources to alleviate the effects of future shortages (see, for example, Brown 1954: chap. 6, Goeller and Weinberg 1976). We believe that the costs of using substitute materials in the future are often underestimated in such studies.

Industrialists, particularly those in the copper industry, and the governments of copper-exporting nations are concerned about the effects of competition from substitutes on the market share of their product. Studies made in response to these concerns usually consider a time span of a few decades and patterns of production and consumption only a little different from current conditions (see, for example, Gluschke, Shaw, and Varon 1979, Slade 1980, Mathur and Clark 1983). Governments of industrial nations, concerned about assured supply in the face of uncertain political conditions, plan for the development of substitutes to circumvent supply dislocations. In response to these concerns the U.S. National Materials Advisory Board (1982) has published a review of the techniques for studying substitution, and the July 1984 issue of the *Annales des Mines* is devoted to a review of efforts at substitution in several industrialized nations.

Our model deals with a much longer time span than any of the studies described above. We therefore preferred to avoid methods of analysis based on calculation of behavioral substitution elasticities (Brown and Field 1979), especially those derived from relatively short spans of experience. Instead, we relied on cost estimates from engineering studies of the costs of manufacture and use of copper-containing products. In principle, the model requires that these costs be evaluated for every product that now contains or may in the future contain copper, but a product-by-product evaluation is much too large a task to undertake in a study of this scope. We needed some scheme for aggregating the uses of copper into a manageable number of classes.

We assumed, for the reasons above, that there will be no entirely new uses of copper for which substitution will occur during the model period. We aggregated all products that use copper into demand categories, in each of which copper provides a specific engineering function, such as the transmission of electrical energy (as in wire). The amount of material required to perform this function was determined by one or a small number of material characteristics, such as electrical conductivity, which we called the ruling properties. Examples of ruling properties are shown in Table 3.1. Alternative materials can be used to obtain equivalent services in each demand category, in amounts determined by the ruling properties. Of these alternatives we considered only the lowest-cost abundant material. Our ultimate objective was to calculate a *switch price* of copper for each demand category; when the price of copper rises above the switch price, the substitute material replaces copper as the means of providing the specific service.

Time Required

In practice, of course, substitution does not occur as soon as the switch price is reached. The engineering required to redesign the product is sel-

Table 3.1   Examples of ruling properties

Demand category	Ruling properties
Heat exchangers	Thermal conductivity
Motors, generators, and transformers	Electrical conductivity, ease of joining with solder
Pipe	Ductility, corrosion resistance, ease of joining
Power transmission wire	Electrical conductivity
Communication wire	Electrical conductivity, ease of joining
Machinery	Strength, machinability, corrosion resistance
Chemical	Toxicity

dom completed beforehand and experience demonstrating the reliability of the product containing substitute material is most unlikely to exist. Switching back and forth between copper and substitutes in response to price changes occurs now in a few products, such as medium-sized electrical motors, but in many of the categories considered in our model substitution will occur for the first time and perhaps after a significant delay. Lyneis (1982) has described the factors that determine how fast the introduction of a substitute actually takes place in an industrial situation today, but to use these factors to determine the actual path of substitution in specific products in our model would require more detailed analysis than is practical.

A useful simplification is possible. Fisher and Pry (1971) found that the progress of substitution in a large number of twentieth-century examples— the replacement of the open hearth by the electric furnace for making specialty steels or the replacement of natural rubber by synthetic, for example—can be represented by a logistic curve relating the fraction of the substitute material used, f, to time. They used the interval between $f = 0.1$ and $f = 0.9$ as a measure of the time required for substitution and found, for substitutions involving metals, intervals ranging from 20 to 40 years. This interval seems not to have changed much throughout the industrial period; for example, the transition time for the replacement of charcoal-produced by coke-produced pig iron in eighteenth-century England also took about 40 years (Gordon 1982). Since the time required to effect substitution of a new material seems to be about the same for a wide range of technologies, we adopted the empirical results of the Fisher-Pry study by constraining the time for switching to new technologies to be no less than 30 years. More precisely, we supposed that a substitution of another material for copper in a given product could be accomplished in at least 30 years, generally starting when the switch price becomes favorable. We interpreted this assumption in terms of investment requirements. New technologies are assumed to be embodied in new capital equipment but, because capital is assumed to have a 30-year lifetime, three decades are required for an older technology to be completely replaced.

Computation of Substitution Costs

The substitution costs in the model include all the costs of making and using a product with an alternative material in such a way that equivalent service is obtained. These costs arise in four different ways.

Materials cost is the cost of the substitute material used less the cost of the original material not used. It is calculated from the unit prices and the amounts of original and substitute materials determined by the ruling-property and equivalent-service principles discussed above.

Design and equipment costs include the cost of redesigning a product when a new material is used in it and the costs of new manufacturing facilities that may be required to make the product from the substitute material. Redesign costs may be substantial in a sophisticated product such as an electric motor. These and equipment costs, encountered when the substitution is first made, may be a barrier to the prompt introduction of a substitute material.

Manufacturing costs are the changes in the cost of manufacturing a product when a substitute material is introduced. They include differences in the costs of the cutting, forming, or joining methods used and in the amounts of other materials included in the product.

Service costs arise from changes in product performance when, as is usually the case, completely equivalent service cannot be obtained from a product made with a substitute material. They could include, for example:

1. Costs that arise from changes in the weight of a product, as in an item that is part of a vehicle.
2. Costs due to altered service life of the product.
3. Costs that arise from failure of the product made of the substitute material to perform as well as expected.

The costs of materials and manufacturing are unit costs and can be expressed in dollars per unit weight of substitute material. We can also express some of the service costs in this way. The costs of contingencies—failure of the new product to perform as expected—may fall on only the fraction of products that actually fail in service, but they must be distributed over all the production to be included in our model. Redesign of a product and new manufacturing equipment represent one-time costs of introducing a substitute material and are not easily incorporated in a strict linear programming framework. We dealt with these costs by including them in the manufacturing category and spreading them evenly over all production of the product containing the substitute material.

The unit cost of substitution, $c_{s,o}$, for substitute material s used in place of original material o in a given product may be expressed as

(3.1) $$c_{s,o} = p_s + c_{m,s} + c_{u,s} - \left(\frac{Q_o}{Q_s}\right)(p_o + c_{m,o} + c_{u,o})$$

where p_s = price of the substitute material ($/kg),

p_o = price of the original material ($/kg),

Q_o = quantity of the original material required to make one unit of the product (kg),

Q_s = quantity of substitute material required to make one unit of the product (kg),

$c_{m,s}$ = manufacturing cost of the product made from substitute material s ($/kg of substitute material),

$c_{m,o}$ = manufacturing cost of the product made from the original material o ($/kg of original material),

$c_{u,s}$ = cost of the use of the product made of the substitute material ($/kg of substitute material),

$c_{u,o}$ = cost of the use of product made of the original material ($/kg of original material).

The tabulated substitution costs are expressed with the aid of the following shorthand notation for the change in the manufacturing and service costs of a given product:

(3.2) $$\Delta c_m = c_{m,s} - \left(\frac{Q_o}{Q_s}\right)c_{m,o},$$

(3.3) $$\Delta c_u = c_{u,s} - \left(\frac{Q_o}{Q_s}\right)c_{u,o}.$$

The cost of substitution, $c_{s,o}$, is expressed in dollars per kilogram of substitute material. The switch price for the use of substitute materials in a product is the price of the original material, $p_{o,s}^*$, that, when inserted as the

Table 3.2 Demand categories

---

1. *Vehicle radiators*: Radiators and heater cores in cars and trucks; radiators in farm machinery, mining equipment, tanks, and other vehicles.
2. *Air conditioning, refrigeration, and heating*: Home and commercial heating and cooling equipment, hot water heating systems, and home refrigerators. (Automobile air conditioners are not included because many have aluminum heat exchangers already.)
3. *Industrial heat exchangers*: Heat exchangers in large-scale industrial applications, such as ship propulsion systems, central power stations, and nuclear reactors.
4. *Power transmission wire*: Electrical-power distribution wire, low-voltage distribution wire, appliance cordage, and control wire. Only insulated wire is included, because aluminum is already used for most bare conductors.
5. *Building wire*: Wire in home and commercial construction.
6. *Electronic wire*: Wire in electronic apparatus including coaxial cable, antenna lead-in wire, hook-up wire, and multiconductor electronic wire and cable.
7. *Motors and generators, <1 HP*: Electric motors, generators, and alternators of less than 1 horsepower.
8. *Motors and generators, 1–20 HP*: Electric motors, generators, and alternators between 1 and 20 horsepower.
9. *Motors and generators, >20 HP*: Electric motors, generators, and alternators of greater than 20 horsepower.
10. *Transformers*: All electric transformers.
11. *Building pipe*: Pipe in home and commercial construction.
12. *Castings*: Copper, brass, and bronze foundry products.
13. *Forgings*: Copper, bronze, and brass forge shop products.
14. *Machined parts*: Copper and copper-based alloy products made by machining (threading, milling, turning, etc.), including plumbing fittings, heating equipment, valves and pipe fittings, screw machine products, nuts, bolts, and washers.
15. *Ordnance*: Guns, gun mountings, and ammunition but not tanks, military vehicles, missiles, or aircraft.
16. *Coinage*: All coins made by the U.S. Mint.
17. *Communication T4*: Long-haul transmission lines, 10,000 circuits per line.
18. *Communication T3*: Long-haul transmission lines, 1,000 circuits per line.
19. *Communication T2*: Short-haul transmission lines, 100 circuits per line.
20. *Communication T1*: Short-haul transmission lines, 24 circuits per line.
21. *Communication local loop*: Local loop transmission lines, 1 circuit per line.

Table 3.3 Copper stock in ten largest demand categories in 1967

Category		Stock	Percentage	Cumulative
Number	Name	(10^6 kg)	of total stock	percentage
4	Power transmission wire	5,519	32	32
5	Building wire	3,220	19	51
10	Transformers	2,162	12	63
11	Pipe	1,554	9	72
9	Motors and generators, >20 HP	912	5	77
2	Air conditioning, refrigeration, and heating	740	4	81
8	Motors and Generators, 1–20 HP	630	4	85
3	Industrial heat exchangers	617	4	89
1	Vehicle radiators	524	3	92
6	Electronic wire	339	2	94

p_o term in Equation (3.1), makes $c_{s,o} = 0$. In our computations, the price p_o is that computed for each time interval in the model.

In principle, the materials model requires that the substitution cost $c_{s,o}$ be computed for every product containing copper today and in the future. We avoided this task by doing the computations for the demand categories defined in terms of ruling properties. The categories used, and the products contained in each category, are listed in Table 3.2. (The amount of copper in the category for chemical properties was too small to have any influence on the model and so we omitted it.)

The amount of copper actually used in the different demand categories ranges widely. Later in this chapter we compute the amount of copper stock in each demand category in 1967. These data yielded the ranked list of the ten largest demand categories in Table 3.3, of which the first five account for more than three-quarters of the copper stock in use in 1967. We expect this pattern to change drastically in the future as substitutes take over more of the services now provided by copper.

Substitution Costs for Copper

In this section we illustrate our methods for computing substitution costs by discussing two examples, the replacement of copper by aluminum in automobile radiators and in electrical wiring for dwellings. We will then summarize our results for the other demand categories.[4]

Vehicle radiators. Aluminum already replaces copper in radiators in some motor vehicles. The heat transfer effected by a radiator depends on the temperature difference between the engine coolant and the air and on the thermal resistance of the radiator. This resistance is the sum of the resistances of the boundary layers at the fluid-metal and the air-metal interfaces and the thermal resistance of the metal wall of the radiator, which depends on the thickness of the metal and its thermal conductivity. The thermal conductivity of aluminum is 54 percent less than that of copper, so an aluminum radiator must be bigger than a copper one to perform the same service. We estimated the required size increase by assuming that the operating temperatures, fluid flow characteristics, and wall thicknesses of the two radiators were the same and that heat flow through the metal walls rather than through the boundary layers determined the amount of heat transfer.[5] Thermal conductivity is the ruling property in this application. The surface area of a radiator made of aluminum must be 1.9 times greater than that of a copper radiator to provide the same service. The aluminum radiator is larger but, because of the lower density of aluminum, it weighs 44 percent less.

The difference in materials cost, $p_s - (Q_o/Q_s)p_o$, has favored the use of aluminum in automobile radiators for almost thirty years, but only a small amount of substitution has taken place. One reason advanced for the reluctance to change is the high cost of the new plant and equipment required (Tilton 1980:138). Once this plant and equipment were in place, however, its cost would be spread over a very large number of units and a long period of time. We do not think this cost would influence the results of our model calculations much. Several manufacturers of radiators have given us estimates of the costs of making aluminum and copper radiators, and on the basis of these it appears that, with the necessary plant and equipment in place, manufacturing costs would be about the same. Hence, $\Delta c_m = 0$.

Additional costs do exist, however, that make the use of aluminum unattractive as a substitute material in radiators. Since an aluminum radiator is larger than the copper one it replaces, the principle of efficient design requires that a compensating increase be made in the size of the vehicle. The greater amount of steel needed for the increase would result in a net increase in the car's weight of about 8 kilograms (after allowing for the lighter weight of the aluminum radiator). From the known relationship between fuel consumption and vehicle weight, we estimate that for a five-year vehicle life and fuel cost of $0.25 per liter, the increase in operating cost of a vehicle equipped with an aluminum radiator will be $2.24 per kilogram of aluminum. Aluminum radiators are much more susceptible than copper to damage from pitting corrosion, both from exposure to rain and salt and from contact with the coolant. Once damaged, they are more costly to repair (Tilton 1980:136). We have added to the cost of using an aluminum radiator 25 percent of our estimate of the manufacturing cost of a radiator to allow for these additional service costs.

The components of the cost of substitution of aluminum for copper in vehicle radiators (all expressed in dollars per kilogram of aluminum) are, then, $p_s = 1.17$, $p_o = 1.45$, $c_m = 0$, and $c_u = 2.24 + 0.33$. Since $Q_o/Q_s = 1.78$, we find that $c_s = \$1.16$ per kilogram of aluminum. According to this analysis, there will have to be a further rise in the price of copper relative to the price of aluminum before this substitution is economically favorable.

Building wire. Aluminum is the only abundant substitute for copper that can be used in applications in which electrical conductivity is the ruling property. Because aluminum has a lower conductivity than copper, a larger wire must carry the same current, more insulating material is required to cover it, and more space is required to house it. Aluminum wire is easier to draw than copper wire, so the manufacturing cost is lower. All these cost increments can be calculated with considerable confidence (Gordon and Hummel 1982).

Aluminum was first used as a substitute for copper in electrical wiring in dwellings in the 1960s because aluminum wire was less expensive than copper wire; between 1.5 and 2.0 million homes had all-aluminum wiring by 1972 (Newman 1975). This substitution was made without evaluation of cost increments that might arise from differences in performance of copper and aluminum wire. By 1970 experience had shown that a severe safety problem existed in many aluminum-wired homes owing to overheating in wall receptacles, switches, and junction and panel boxes. Temperatures high enough to ignite adjacent wood were attained, and a number of serious fires resulted.

Four factors contribute to excessive heat generation at junctions between aluminum and other metals carrying electric current (Mittleman 1969, National Bureau of Standards 1974). These are high electrical resistance due to failure to break the oxide film on the aluminum wire when a mechanical joint is made; creep of the aluminum wire in mechanical joints, resulting in loss of contact pressure; expansion of the aluminum wire due to heating, which causes accelerated creep; and electrolytic corrosion at contacts between dissimilar metals. Junction failures are a consequence of the physical properties of aluminum, which are different from those of copper; the rapid formation of a hard, continuous oxide on a freshly exposed surface; lower melting temperature;[6] and lower yield strength of the pure metal. Satisfactory junctions can be made, but they have to be designed to make allowance for the differences in properties of aluminum and copper.

The cost of repairing an increased number of failed junctions should be counted as part of the cost of substituting aluminum for copper wire. One method of estimating this cost is to use data for the number of repairs and replacements determined from a sample of homes built in 1969–70 (Franklin Institute 1979). From these data we estimate the present discounted cost of the repairs to be $4.35 per kilogram of aluminum. This cost may be avoided in the future; it could have been avoided in the past by proper design, in which case the cost of the design work and the new installation procedures required would have been added to the cost of manufacturing. If anything, our evaluation of the cost of using aluminum as a substitute for copper wiring is an underestimate; no allowance has been made for the cost of wiring out of service or for the cost of lives and property lost in the fires that resulted from the failures of the aluminum wiring systems.

Substitution costs in the model. In Table 3.4 we list the substitution costs applied in the model calculations. Our results show that the cost of the substitute material itself is but one of the factors determining the substitution cost; the costs associated with the manufacture and use of the product containing the substitute material are often much more important. The most expensive substitute for copper is titanium, which was proposed as a replacement for copper-based alloys in industrial heat exchangers because of its superior corrosion resistance. Its use requires a large increment in manufacturing cost because of the difficulty of fabricating titanium tubing; substitution becomes attractive only if there are corresponding use savings through longer life, greater reliability, and reduced maintenance of the condenser. The lower efficiency of electric motors made with aluminum rather than copper conductors becomes more important with increasing size and makes the use of the substitute quite unattractive for the largest class of motors. A high substitution cost has been assigned to the electronic wire category, on the basis of the ease with which copper wires can be joined by soldering. We found it particularly difficult to make reliable estimates of this substitution cost, and this category may well be thought of as a proxy for all industrial uses of copper that are particularly valuable. We investigate the dependence of the model on this particular cost estimate in the sensitivity analyses discussed in the next chapter.

Reliability of the Cost Estimates

Substitution of alternative materials occurs on a case-by-case basis; designers recast each product in which a substitute might be used and a detailed engineering study is used to evaluate the cost of using the new material. Because copper appears in such a wide variety of products that a case-by-case study of substitution costs was impossible for our model, we have used the aggregation of products on the basis of ruling properties and the principle of efficient design to make estimates of substitution costs. How reliable are these estimates?

The ruling properties are easiest to identify in the electrical applications, where copper is chosen for its high conductivity, and more difficult in categories in which copper affords a combination of properties not duplicated by any single substitute material. In the "machined parts" category, for example, a combination of strength, corrosion resistance, and ease of fabrication governs the selection of materials. The ruling properties determine how much substitute material must be used in each category to obtain equivalent service. The actual cost of materials is probably the most reliable part of our estimates, but as we have seen it is usually unimportant compared with changes that arise in the cost of manufacturing and using a product after the introduction of substitutes. These costs are evaluated on the basis of redesign of the product as required by the ruling properties and are most reliable in the demand categories characterized by one ruling property. Fortunately, in the categories that account for 94 percent of the copper in use (Table 3.3), a single ruling property is easiest to identify.

We developed two methods for determining manufacturing costs, one of which relies on experts' estimates for specific products in the relevant industries. These are of course not as useful for those categories that contain many different products; the method works better for the category of heat exchangers than for machined parts. Our other method relied on product census data. We subtracted the aggregate cost of materials from the aggregate cost of all products in one of the census categories—copper castings, for example—to find the manufacturing cost for all the products in the category. We then did the same for a category containing similar products made of the substitute material—stainless steel castings, for example—to find the difference in manufacturing cost. A disadvantage of this method is that it reveals nothing about why the costs differ as they do. One indication of the general reliability of the cost estimates is the agreement between the results of the two methods in those cases where both could be used.

Table 3.4 Substitution cost data[a]

Demand category	1967 copper stock (10^6 kg)	Substitute material	p_o (1978 $/kg)	p_s (1978 $/kg)	$Q_{o,i}/Q_{s,i}$ (kg Cu/kg sub)	Δc_m (1978 $/kg sub)	Δc_u (1978 $/kg sub)	$c_{s,o}$ (1978 $/kg sub)
1. Vehicle radiators	524	Aluminum	1.45	1.17	1.78	0	2.24	1.16
2. Air conditioners, refrigeration, and heating	740.4	Aluminum	1.45	1.17	1.78	0	0.13	−1.28
3. Industrial heat exchangers	616.9	Titanium	1.45	17.32	0.103	114.85	−108.45	10.00
4. Power transmission cable	5519	Aluminum	1.45	1.17	2.08	−8.69	7	−3.54
5. Building wire	3220	Aluminum	1.45	1.17	2.08	−8.69	4.34	−6.19
6. Electronic wire	339	Aluminum	1.45	1.17	2.08	382	0	380.15
7. Motors and generators, <1 HP	173.0	Aluminum	1.45	1.17	2.89	43.15	15.82	55.95
8. Motors and generators, 1–20 HP	629.9	Aluminum	1.45	1.17	2.89	44.36	161	202.34
9. Motors and generators, >20 HP	912	Aluminum	1.45	1.17	2.89	55.77	225	277.75

No.									
10.	Transformers	Aluminum	2162.6	1.45	1.17	2.08	0.975	0.975	0.10
11.	Building pipe	Plastic	1554.6	1.45	0.08	1.49	1.04	1.21	0.17
12.	Castings	Stainless steel	294.8	1.45	2.67	2.8	18.38	-2.39	14.60
13.	Forgings	Stainless steel	56	1.45	2.67	1.7	-0.51	-0.44	-0.75
14.	Machined parts	Stainless steel	246.9	1.45	2.67	2.8	12.8	-3.15	7.54
15.	Ordnance	Carbon steel	29.7	1.45	0.35	1.9	3.66	0	1.26
16.	Coinage	Zinc		1.45	0.68	1.26	0	1.20	0.05
17.	Communication T4	Glass	0.1	1.45	0.1	1.0	667	0	666.55
18.	Communication T3	Glass	0.13	1.45	0.1	1.0	372.1	0	370.75
19.	Communication T2	Glass	0.16	1.45	0.1	1.0	66.9	0	65.55
20.	Communication T1	Glass	3.87	1.45	0.1	1.0	22.35	0	21.00
21.	Communication LL	Glass	116	1.45	0.1	1.0	19.99	0	18.64

a. See Equation (3.1) for definitions of symbols used.

Differences in the cost of using a product are more difficult to estimate accurately than costs of manufacturing. The case studies we have carried out show that such cost differences spread widely through the economy and can arise in many ways. Some examples are changes in the efficiency of energy use by the product (as in electrical motors and transformers), changes in the service life of the product (as in an electric motor operating at a higher temperature as a result of being wound with aluminum wire), and changes in the weight or bulk of a product that affect its fuel consumption (as in automobile radiators). We can estimate these cost changes from engineering data, but because they are so dispersed, some components of the change in the cost of use may be overlooked in our analyses.

The costs of failures in service of substitute-containing products can be estimated only when actual experience exists. They can be quite large, as was the case when aluminum replaced copper in electrical wiring for dwellings. We see no reason to suppose that similar failures will not occur in the future, and again we think we have underestimated rather than overestimated the costs that are likely to result.

Despite these uncertainties, we believe that for the purposes of the copper model our substitution-cost calculations are a useful guide to the amount of substitution that will occur. Because we have employed a wide range of different case studies and different methods of estimation, it is unlikely that an error concerning a specific detail of a product containing a substitute will cause the overall results of the model calculations to be seriously distorted.

Recycling

As products wear out and are removed from service the metal they contain can be recycled, provided it has not been dissipated in such a way that it cannot be recovered, as by corrosion. If a product is not recycled directly, it may be placed in a scrap pile from which the metal it contains can be recovered at a later time. Although recycling has been practiced for as long as metals have been used, much more metal has been dissipated than recovered; today less than 20 percent of all the metal that has ever been mined remains in use or available for reuse (NATO 1976:27). Increased scarcity of new sources of metal will change this proportion in the future.

Costs

The metal-producing industry itself generates a substantial amount of scrap. "Home scrap," "prompt scrap," or "runaround scrap" is easy to recycle within the smelter or finishing mill where it is produced. Scrap, such as metal chips, produced during the manufacture of finished products is called new scrap. Since it is made at a concentrated source and is easily segregated by type of metal, it is likely to be recycled. Scrap obtained from products that have been withdrawn from service is called old scrap. The copper industry today recycles almost twice as much new scrap as old scrap (NATO 1976:89). Unfortunately, published estimates of the amount of recycling often do not clearly distinguish among home, new, and old scrap. We assume in the copper model that all home and new scrap is reused; we consider recycling only of old scrap.

Substantial amounts of copper are used in capital equipment and structures, in which the lifetime of copper-containing products is relatively long and the chances for recovery relatively good. At present, old scrap supplies about 25 percent of the copper consumed in the United States. Estimates of the amount of scrap available and the fraction actually recycled vary considerably. About 75 percent of the copper in use is thought to be available for future recycling, while estimates of the fraction now being recycled range from 31 to 60 percent (Bever 1976, NATO 1976:36). The amount recycled depends on the cost of recovering the old scrap relative to the cost of new metal. There are many repositories of old products that will be recycled when the price of copper becomes high enough. It is estimated, for example, that 1.5 million kilograms of unused copper cable lies beneath New York City and has not been recycled because of the high cost of recovering it from tunnels and conduits (NATO 1976:35).

We based our estimates of the amount of metal recycled on the amount of copper already in use, the lifetimes of the various copper-containing products, and the cost of recycling. Recycling cost includes three components, the costs of collection, separation, and refining.

Collection cost is the cost of gathering discarded products and bringing them to a recycling center. The more widely dispersed the product, the more its collection will cost. For example, it is relatively easy to bring obsolete railway locomotives to a scrap yard, more difficult to collect worn cars and farm machinery, and very difficult to salvage ships lost in the deep ocean.

Separation cost. Copper dispersed within a product or interconnected with other materials will cost more to recycle than copper that can be recovered in massive pieces. Bus bars from a power plant are easy to extract for remelting, but the copper windings from a motor or generator have to be separated from an iron frame and from insulation before they can be reprocessed. Redesign of products to facilitate separation during scrapping of the different metals they contain would lower the cost of recycling but would generate new manufacturing and use costs analogous to those included in the cost of substitution.

Refining costs. Usually home scrap and new scrap need only be remelted to be reused (Bever 1976), whereas old scrap may have to be refined before it has properties equivalent to those of new metal. The cost of this refining depends on the admixture of foreign material. Low-grade old scrap (less than 99.5 percent copper) is usually processed in small blast-furnace plants dedicated to secondary metal production (Biswas and Davenport 1980:362).

In theory all scrap copper is recoverable. In practice some uses disperse the metal so widely that the scrap is a lower-grade resource than lean ore. Copper that corrodes and then enters groundwater, for example, is dispersed beyond practical recovery. We have assumed for the purposes of the model that 20 percent of the copper in use will never be recycled because it is more widely dispersed, and hence of lower grade, than the backstop resource (copper-containing silicate rock).

In a model of copper recycling, each copper-containing product would be assigned a recovery cost determined by the nature of the product and its degree of dispersion. The product categories might include, for example, urban automobiles, rural automobiles, wiring in satellites, and so on. Unfortunately, there is nothing equivalent to our ruling properties with which to set up categories that would facilitate determination of recycling costs. The number of categories would have to be large, because of the need to consider on a case-by-case basis the nature of each product containing copper and the way in which it was used in estimating recycling costs, metal contents, and product lifetimes. Instead of attempting such detailed studies, we have distributed the scrap copper available in the United States among six categories, five of which have been used by the U.S. Bureau of Mines to determine recycling rates and service lives for the years 1961–1970 (Carrillo, Hibpsham, and Rosenkranz 1974): building construction, transportation, consumer and general, industrial machinery and equipment, and electrical. The sixth category is coinage.

For our calculations we needed to estimate the amount of recycling in each of the demand categories. Hence we had to determine the amount of copper, the product life, and the recycling cost for the recycling categories and then incorporate these into the demand categories for use in the computations. Table 3.5 shows how we distributed copper quantities between the recycling and the demand categories.

Delivery of copper to the recycling categories depends on the service lives of the products in the categories. Slade [1980a:131] has determined an average lifetime of 17 years for copper-containing products today. We expect that in the future less copper and more substitutes will be used in products with relatively short service lives, such as American automobiles, whereas products with long useful lives, such as large motors and generators, are more likely to be made with copper as before. Hence we have taken the average product life to be 30 years, or three of the ten-year computation periods used in the model.

The amount of copper contained in each recycling category is related to the flow of copper in the model by

$$(3.4) \qquad S(q,n) = S(q,n-1) + \sum_{m} F(q,m) \, C(m,n-3) - Y(q,n),$$

where $S(q,n)$ = the amount of copper metal in recycling category q at the end of period n,

$C(m,n-3)$ = amount of copper metal delivered to demand category m in period $(n-3)$,

$F(q,m)$ = the fraction of copper scrapped from demand category m that goes to recycling category q,

$Y(q,n)$ = the amount of copper metal recycled from recycling category q in period n.

This equation states that the available stock of copper in each recycling category is the amount of metal that was left at the end of the previous period plus the amount that was delivered to that category in period n, less the amount recycled. Note that by "delivered" we do not mean that the product or its contained copper is physically placed in a scrap heap; the cost of recycling includes the cost of collecting the product from wherever it was last used as well as the cost of extracting copper from it.

Each category will include some products from which copper is easily recycled and some for which recycling will be very costly (compare an automobile abandoned in the Bronx with one abandoned on the Alaska Highway). The marginal cost of recovering copper will rise with the frac-

Table 3.5 Distribution of copper between recycling and demand categories

Demand category	Percentage not recyclable	Building construction	Transportation	Consumer and general	Industrial machinery	Electrical and electronic	Coinage
Vehicle radiators	20	—	80	—	—	—	—
Air conditioning and refrigeration	20	26.7	—	26.7	26.7	—	—
Industrial heat exchangers	20	—	—	—	80	—	—
Power wire	20	4	4	—	36	36	—
Building wire	20	80	—	—	—	—	—
Electronic wire	20	—	20	20	20	20	—
Motors, <1 HP	20	—	8	56	8	8	—
Motors, >1 HP	20	—	20	20	20	20	—
Transformers	20	—	—	16	—	64	—
Building pipe	20	80	—	—	—	—	—
Castings	20	24	—	—	56	—	—
Forgings	20	24	—	—	56	—	—
Machine parts	20	16	16	16	16	16	—
Ordnance	20	—	—	80	—	—	—
Coinage	20	—	—	—	—	—	80
Communication T4	20	—	—	—	—	80	—
Communication T3	20	—	—	—	—	80	—
Communication T2	20	—	—	—	—	80	—
Communication T1	20	—	—	—	—	80	—
Communication LL	20	—	—	—	—	80	—

tion of copper in each category that is actually recycled. The fraction of the metal that is recycled in each category will depend on the price of copper; as the price rises, the fraction recycled will increase. Since we have not been able to find data to define the relationship between cost and fraction recycled, we have assumed a simple functional form relating recycling cost to fraction recycled. This relation is illustrated in Figure 3.1 and can be expressed analytically as

(3.5) $$C_q = d_q + a_q \left(\frac{f_q}{0.8 - f_q}\right),$$

where C_q = marginal cost of recycling metal from recycling category q,

f_q = fraction of recoverable scrap metal in recycling category q that is recovered,

a_q, d_q = constants to be determined.

We evaluated the coefficients in this equation by fitting the function to data on recycling published by Carrillo, Hibpsham, and Rosenkranz (1974), who also provide data on the amount of copper in products becoming obsolete each year from 1961 to 1970 and the amount of copper recycled each year. Coinage is not considered in their study so we made use of data from the 1978 annual report of the director of the Mint; 27.5×10^3 kilograms of copper coins were removed from circulation in fiscal 1978 while 38.0×10^6 kilograms of copper coins were produced.

When we calculated the fraction of copper recycled from products be-

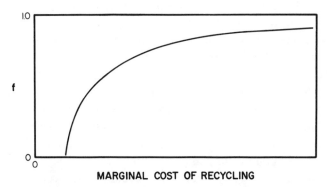

Figure 3.1   The fraction f of copper recycled in a given category represented as a function of the marginal cost of recycling.

coming obsolete each year for each recycling category and compared these with the price of copper, we found that the correlation between the marginal cost of recycling and the fraction recycled was poor. The most likely reason for the difference is that the time required for the recycling industry to respond to changes in the price of copper is much longer than a year. Hence the data for the years 1961–1970 were used to compute average amounts of recycling for the entire period. Because there are only enough data to determine one unknown coefficient in the recycling equation above, we set $d_q = 0$. We assumed that C_q is determined by a competitive market and took it to be the average real price of copper from 1961 to 1970 expressed in 1978 dollars. The results appear in Table 3.6. We find that a_q is low for the industrial and electrical categories, where products tend to be large and concentrated in industrial establishments from which they are easily delivered to scrap yards, and high for the consumer uses, where the products are smaller, more numerous, and more dispersed. Coinage is unusual because it is a single-product category; the low amount of recycling may reflect the high degree of dispersion of copper coins.

Reliability of the Results

The recycling rates presented in Table 3.6 are estimated from a limited set of data and could be improved if more information about recycling were available in a wider range of categories over a longer period of time. They extrapolate experience from a time when interest in recycling was low and may not be a good guide to future costs. For example, recycling costs can be influenced by public policy decisions on waste disposal practices; if recycling were to become a by-product of the operation of more efficient waste disposal systems, recycling costs would be lowered. Recycling costs could also be reduced by the redesign of products to make recovery of their metal content easier, but this would introduce new manufacturing and use costs. Further analysis of these possibilities did not seem worthwhile, because the model results are not very sensitive to recycling costs (see p. 117) and the amount of recycling is always limited to less than the metal already in service. As long as demand for copper grows, as the model shows it will, recycling can make only a limited contribution to its supply. The effects of substantial changes in our estimates of recycling costs were examined in the sensitivity analyses discussed in Chapter 5.

Table 3.6 Calculation of the constant a_q from average data, 1961–1970, and Bureau of the Mint data for 1978, d = \$0.25/kg

Recycling category	Copper recovered (10^3 short tons)[a]	Copper becoming obsolete (10^3 short tons)	f_q[b]	a_q (\$/kg)[c]
Building construction	880.7	2,924.4	0.301	0.45
Transportation	883.1	2,919.9	0.302	0.45
Consumer and general	393.8	2,175.3	0.181	0.88
Industrial machinery	1,672.8	4,570.0	0.366	0.34
Electrical and electronic	1,605.1	3,444.6	0.466	0.22
Coinage[d]	30.37	4,189.6	0.00725	164.0

a. Table 3, USBM–IC8622, Coinage from Bureau of the Mint.

b. (Copper recovered)/(copper available for recovery).

c. Calculated for a marginal cost of \$0.44/kg, except for coinage where, since 1978 prices were used, the price is \$1.45/kg.

d. Table A-8, USBM–IC8622, Coinage from Bureau of the Mint.

Demand Categories

In other studies of resource scarcity, demand has been described in terms of product or industrial categories, but we have found functional categories of demand more useful for the purposes of our model. We believe that, over the long run, the amount of copper used in the economy will be more closely related to its ruling properties in various applications—that is, to the purpose it serves—than to the particular items of equipment in which it is embodied. For example, about 10 kilograms of copper are used in an automobile, of which about 5 kilograms are used in a heat exchanger (the radiator) and most of the rest in motors and generators. In the traditional method of describing demand, all copper in automobiles would be placed in one category, thereby lumping together all the different uses of copper in automobiles. In our approach the copper in the radiators of automobiles is aggregated with the copper in small heat exchangers in all other products that require this service, the copper in electrical motors and generators in automobiles is aggregated with that in all other similar-sized motors and generators, and so forth.

We used functional rather than product demand categories because, in the long run, the time path of substitution will be more similar across functional categories than across product categories. We expect, for example, the time path of substitution for copper in the heat exchangers of electrical power plants will more nearly resemble that in large heat exchangers in other industries than that in other copper uses, such as power transmission wire, in the electric-power industry. The major difficulty we faced was that most data on economic activity are presented in terms of specific products or industries rather than the functions served by particular materials.

A second respect in which our approach differs is in the distinction we make between stocks and flows. A stock is the amount of material, copper or substitutes in our case, on hand and committed to some specific use at a given time. A flow is the time rate of change of a stock and we call the ultimate unit of demand for flow copper-equivalent services, which is all those production or consumption activities in which copper is currently used, even though substitutes may be used for the same purpose in the future. Put differently, copper-equivalent services are a flow or stream, but this flow is produced by a variety of inputs, such as labor, energy, and the services of the stock of copper-equivalent capital. The demand for new copper-equivalent capital (that is, the demand either for new copper or for copper substitutes) then requires additions to the stock of copper-equivalent capital—capital that may include aluminum, plastics, and other substitutes along with copper itself.

As an example, consider demand for telecommunications services. Providing a certain amount and configuration of these services of a given quality requires a certain stock of transmission facilities. As the demand for services increases, the required stock of transmission facilities also increases. Depending on which costs less, the increased demand for telecommunications services may be met either by the use of copper or of substitutes for copper, such as radios, satellites, or lightguides. To the extent that the increased stock of transmission facilities is supplied by the use of copper, there would be an increase in copper capital that would require deliveries of copper. But to the extent that substitutes such as lightguides or satellites are used, more of what we call the copper capital would be made up of substitutes.

Table 3.7   Summary of demand data

Demand categories (major and subdivisions)	Estimated copper consumption[a]			
	1967[b]	1967[c]	1972[c]	1977[c]
Heat exchangers	430.52			
1. Vehicle radiators		117	138	213
2. Air conditioning/refrigeration		165.5	311.5	317.7
3. Industrial heat exchangers		53.1	41.9	21.3
Power wire	1,380.9			
4. Power transmission cable		538.1	598.1	611.4
5. Building wire		456.5	570.4	658.6
6. Electronic wire		77.4	51.6	99.6
Motors, generators, etc.	731.2			
7. <1/20 HP		46.0	52.6	52.7
8. 1/20 to 20 HP		94.6	108.0	108.3
9. >20 HP		84.0	89.0	96.2
10. Transformers		157.7	139.2	83.3
Pipe	388.52			
11. Building pipe		n.a.[d]	n.a.	327.8
Machinery	392.37			
12. Castings		405.0	366.7	567.8
13. Forgings		56.8	60.2	76.6
14. Machined parts		444.2	486.6	564.2
15. Ordnance		246.3	155.7	67.6
Communications	176.5			
16. T4 (high capacity)				
17. T3				
18. T2		n.a.	n.a.	736.0
19. T1 (low capacity)				
20. Local loop				
Total	3,500	3,801	4,094	4,602.1

Source: Nordhaus, Gordon, and Hummel 1982.
a. In millions of pounds.
b. Estimates for major categories from input-output tables.
c. Estimates from census data.
d. Data not available.

We divided the annual consumption of copper services in the United States into seven final-demand categories with the aid of data from the 1967 input-output table of total requirements. The categories were heat exchangers; electric wire; motors, generators, and transformers; pipe; machinery; communications; and "other," a catch-all category for those copper-using industries that do not fall into any of the other categories. We distributed copper consumption in this last category over the other six in proportion to their annual consumption of copper services. The distribution of copper consumption across the six categories is shown in column 2 of Table 3.7.

We next subdivided the six categories into more detailed subcategories for which substitution possibilities can be estimated. Our twenty detailed subdivisions appear in column 1 of Table 3.7. Copper consumption for each of these subdivisions was derived from census data; we used the three most recent years for which data are available, 1967, 1972, and 1977. The results appear in columns 3, 4, and 5 of the table. We then adjusted the data for 1967 to the control totals from column 2 in order to obtain final estimates of demand for copper-equivalent services that are consistent with total deliveries of copper.[7]

We projected the demand for copper-equivalent services into the future by assuming a unitary income elasticity and zero price elasticity.[8] These assumptions were necessary because of the complete lack of data from which to estimate the elasticities. Note, however, that the census data show that the share of copper services in the cost of final products is quite low, in all cases below 1 percent. A doubling of the price of copper will increase the price of an automobile by only 0.1 percent. Therefore, as long as the services are essential to the product (as they are, for example, in wire used for the transmission of electric power), any price sensitivity of the final product to the price of copper is likely to be minimal.

Finally, the key assumption driving the future growth in demand for copper services arises from our assumption of growth in GNP, or national output. For the purposes of the model we assumed that there will be an era of relatively high economic growth—one in which the GNP increases at 3 percent per annum—for the first 100 years of the model period and that thereafter the growth rate will slow to an annual rate of 1 percent. The discount rate (or real interest rate, the interest rate corrected for inflation) is 8 percent during the 100 years of high economic growth and 4 percent during the subsequent years.

4 Equations and Computations for the Copper Model

After having described the various factors influencing the demand and supply of copper, we are now ready to present the copper model and the results of our calculations. In this chapter we lay out the algebraic structure of the copper model and introduce the objective function to be minimized and the constraints (or inequalities) that are built into the computer program. The purpose of this chapter is to allow the specialists to understand exactly what procedure we followed. For those interested only in the results, or who are reluctant to struggle with mathematical models, little of substance will be lost by moving directly to Chapters 5 and 6.

The Variables

We begin with a careful description of the variables employed in our copper model. Table 4.1 assigns notations to the various categories of the model: ore grades, possible substitutes for copper in its various uses, and demand categories already described in Chapter 3. Tables 4.2, 4.3, and 4.4 list the variables whose interrelations are examined in the model.

A distinction is made between *exogenous* and *endogenous* variables. The exogenous variables, listed in Tables 4.2 and 4.3, are determined outside the model—by nature, by technological feasibility, or by economic practice. They have in turn been subdivided into two subsets. Table 4.2 lists first the costs of extraction (that is, of mining and refining) of copper from deposits of various grades; next, the costs associated with the use of various substitutes in the pertinent use categories of copper, expressed in 1978 dollars per kilogram of the substitute brought into use; and, third, the cost of recycling copper from the various recycling categories.

Table 4.3 contains all other exogenous variables included in the model. The first, denoted $\overline{R}(j)$, specifies the total copper resources of grade j extractable as of 1970. Two more exogenous variables, $\overline{E}(k,m)$ and $\overline{F}(q,m)$, are primarily technological. $\overline{E}(k,m)$ is a substitution-efficiency factor; it

Table 4.1   Categories and notation for the copper allocation model

Categories	Indexes[a]
Grades of copper deposits	$j = 1, \ldots, \bar{j} \equiv 22$
Substitute materials	$k = 1, \ldots, \bar{k} \equiv 7$
Demand categories	$m = 1, \ldots, \bar{m} \equiv 21$
Periods (decades): 1940–1949, 1950–1959, 1960–1969, 1970–1979, 1980–1989, . . . , 2140–2149	$n = \begin{cases} -2, -1, 0, \\ 1, 2, \ldots, \bar{n} \equiv 18 \end{cases}$
Recycling categories	$q = 1, \ldots, \bar{q} \equiv 24$

a. The bars over indexes indicate the maximum values (that is, $\bar{j} = 22 \equiv$ index of lowest-grade ore).

Table 4.2   Cost variables of copper model[a]

Symbol	Definition	Unit
$\bar{C}^x(j)$	Cost of extraction (mining and refining) of copper from deposit of grade j	Dollars per kg (1978 prices) per kg copper extracted
$\bar{C}^a(k,m)$	Cost of using substitute k (such as aluminum) in demand category m	Dollars per kg (1978 prices) per kg of substitute
$\bar{C}^y(q)$	Cost of recycling copper from recycling category q	Dollars per kg (1978 prices) per kg copper recycled

a. The overbars on C, the cost variable, indicate that all cost levels are deemed exogenous.

indicates the quantity of a substitute required to replace a given quantity of copper. As a denominator $\bar{E}(k,m)$ converts any given quantity of substitute k (for instance, the quantity denoted $A(k,m,n)$ in Table 4.4) into the amount of copper, denoted $A(k,m,n)/\bar{E}(k,m)$, required to provide equivalent services to demand category m. We explain its use in Equation (4.6) below.

Table 4.3   Other exogenous variables

Symbol	Definition	Unit
$\overline{R}(j)$	Estimated U.S. resources of copper of grade j extractable as of 1970	10^6 kg copper
$\overline{E}(k,m)$	Efficiency of substitute k for use in demand category m	kg of substitute k replacing 1 kg copper
$\overline{F}(q,m)$	Fraction of copper scrapped by demand category m allocated to recycling category q; this fraction is the same for all periods n	Pure number $(\Sigma_q \bar{F}(q,m) = 0.8$ for each m)
$\overline{D}(m,n)$	Demand for copper services or copper-equivalent services projected for demand category m in period n	10^6 kg copper or copper-equivalent material in 10 years
$\overline{G}(n)$	Rate of proportional growth of demand in all demand categories in period n	Pure number per annum: 0.03 if $1 \leq n \leq 10$, 0.01 if $11 \leq n \leq 18$
$\overline{I}(n)$	Real interest rate in period n	Pure number per annum

The third exogenous variable in our model, $\overline{F}(q,m)$, as defined in Equation (3.4), specifies the distribution of scrapped copper among the recycling categories. As explained in Chapter 3, we assume a 30-year time interval between delivery of fresh copper to demand category m and the distribution of this same copper into scrap categories labeled $q = 1, \ldots, \bar{q}$. We further assume that only 80 percent of copper can be economically recycled. Hence the sum $\Sigma_{q=1}^{\bar{q}} \overline{F}(q,m)$ adds to the same pure number, 0.8, for all demand categories.

Three of the four remaining items in Table 4.3, $\overline{D}(m,n)$, $\overline{G}(n)$, and $\overline{I}(n)$, express underlying economic assumptions. First, we define the exogenous variable $\overline{D}(m,n)$ on the basis of a postulated growth rate of demand for copper services or copper-equivalent services. Specifically, $\overline{D}(m,n)$ represents the algebraic product of two factors, the first of which, $\overline{D}(m,1)$, gives our estimate of demand for demand category m during the first period. The second factor depends only on the period n, in a way expressed by

$$\overline{D}(m,n) = \overline{D}(m,1) \prod_{h=1}^{n-1} [1 + \overline{G}(h)], \qquad n = 2, \ldots, \overline{n}.$$

Note that the second factor is itself a cumulative product of $(n - 1)$ *per-period growth factors,* $1 + \overline{G}(n)$, where $\overline{G}(n)$ denotes a *per-decade growth rate* of demand, associated with period n but common to all demand categories. Thus, the formula for $\overline{D}(m,n)$ multiplies the demand for use of copper by category m in period 1, $\overline{D}(m,1)$, by a succession of growth factors to obtain demand in period n.

This formula does not specify how $\overline{G}(n)$ depends on n. As a simple yet interesting case, indicated in Table 4.3, the *per-decade* growth rate, $\overline{G}(n)$, has been assumed to remain constant over all the first ten periods and thereafter to drop to a lower constant rate over the remaining seven periods.

Finally, the variable $\overline{I}(n)$ represents the *per-annum* rate of interest for a given decade. This is used as the discount rate whereby costs incurred in future decades are made comparable with those of the decade in question. Note also that the interest rate used here is the "real interest rate," the rate of interest corrected for the rate of inflation; the real interest rate is calculated as the nominal or money interest rate minus the rate of inflation.

Again as indicated in Table 4.3, $\overline{I}(n)$ is postulated to be a constant, denoted $\overline{I}$, for the first ten periods and to fall from there to a constant level equal to one-half the previous level. These jumps are not intended as anticipations of sudden, miraculously foreseeable, economic collapses. Rather—in the spirit of the "if . . . then . . ." approach—they approximate in a transparent way the effects of an expected slowdown in economic growth and in the related interest rate.

Table 4.4 lists one more set of variables, called decision variables. As we explained in Chapter 1, the outcomes represented by the values of these variables are subject to two alternative interpretations: (1) The outcomes are the result of a cost minimization, wherein society operates to minimize the total discounted costs of meeting the demand requirements, subject to the available resources and the existing technology. We might imagine that some omniscient planning body determined the quantities and the efficiency prices, in which case the price and quantity variables shown in Table 4.4 would be the planning variables. (2) More subtle is the interpretation arising from the deep economic theorem that we called the correspondence principle, which states that such a cost minimization is also the outcome of a competitive general equilibrium—that is, an economy in

Table 4.4   Decision variables

Symbol	Decision	Unit
$X(j,n)$	Extraction of copper of grade j in period n	10^6 kg copper in 10 years
$A(k,m,n)$	Amount of copper-substitute type k put into use in demand category m in period n	10^6 kg of copper-substitute in 10 years
$Y(q,n)$	Copper recycled from recycling category q in period n	10^6 kg copper in 10 years
$C(m,n)$	Copper delivered for use in demand category m in period n	10^6 kg copper in 10 years
$U(m,n)$	Stock of copper and copper-equivalent capital in use in demand category m at end of period n	10^6 kg copper or equivalent
$S(q,n)$	Stock of scrap copper in category q at end of period n	10^6 kg of copper

which competitive, profit-maximizing firms supply copper and substitutes in response to prices set on spot and futures markets. Again we stress that, subject to the assumptions outlined in Chapter 1, the variables shown in Table 4.4 can be interpreted in either of the two senses just described.

The decision variables given in Table 4.4 are easily explained by referring to Chapters 2 and 3 above. One distinction, however, is worth noting here. The variables $X(j,n)$, $A(k,m,n)$, $Y(q,n)$, and $C(m,n)$ are all flow variables, in contrast with the stock variables $U(m,n)$ and $S(q,n)$. The difference is indicated by the units that measure the two types: the flow variables are expressed in terms of quantity per period, whereas the stock variables are quantities in existence at some point in time, say, at the beginning or end of a period.

Recall that the flow variables do *not* represent the variability of the flow within the time period. Instead, to simplify the model, we assumed the flows in any decade remain constant throughout the ten-year period. Between successive decades, of course, variations of flows are allowed.

The Equations

We next present the objective function and the constraints of the copper model. Roughly speaking, we wish to calculate the allocation of copper resources that minimizes the costs of meeting a given projected path of demands for copper-equivalent services. More precisely, we want to minimize the minimand M, where

(4.1) $$M \equiv \sum_{n=1}^{\bar{n}} \overline{DF}(n) \cdot \overline{TC}(n).$$

In this expression $\overline{DF}(n)$ is a discount factor per decade for period n, defined as

(4.2) $$\overline{DF}(n) \equiv \begin{cases} (1 + \bar{I})^{-10n} & \text{if } 1 \leq n \leq 10, \\ (1 + \bar{I})^{-100} \cdot (1 + \tfrac{1}{2}\bar{I})^{-10(n-10)} & \text{if } 10 < n \leq \bar{n} = 18, \end{cases}$$

and $\overline{TC}(n)$ is total cost—the cost of extraction, substitution (in this case, by aluminum), and recycling—calculated as

(4.3) $$\overline{TC}(n) \equiv \sum_{j=1}^{\bar{j}} \overline{C}^x(j) \cdot X(j,n) + \sum_{k=1}^{\bar{k}} \sum_{m=1}^{\bar{m}} \overline{C}^a(k,m) \cdot A(k,m,n)$$

$$+ \sum_{q=1}^{\bar{q}} \overline{C}^y(q) \cdot Y(q,n).$$

These expressions state how the total cost of any program of extraction and recycling of copper, and of its substitution by other materials, depends on the numerical values of the three decision variables $X(j,n)$, $A(k,m,n)$, and $Y(q,n)$. The total cost-minimizing values are to be determined for all three variables with reference to all future periods labeled $n = 1, \ldots, \bar{n}$; for the extraction variable also with regard to all grades $j = 1, \ldots, \bar{j}$ of copper that may be extracted; for the substitution variable with regard to all potential substitutes of copper $k = 1, \ldots, \bar{k}$ and to be used in any demand category $m = 1, \ldots, \bar{m}$; and, finally, for the recycling variable with regard to any recycling that may be carried out from any scrap heap $q = 1, \ldots, \bar{q}$.

Given the total cost in a given period, $\overline{TC}(n)$, to obtain comparability of costs for different periods we multiply each period's cost by a corresponding discount factor, here defined as $\overline{DF}(n)$. The minimand M is the sum over all periods of the discounted total costs. The minimand is a *linear* function of decision variables, with exogenous variables serving as coefficients.

The minimization of costs shown in Equations (4.1)–(4.3) is constrained by resource availability, technology, and demand. We now present the constraints—five sets in all—operating in the copper model.

The Constraints

Resource Availability

(4.4) $$\sum_{n=1}^{\bar{n}} X(j,n) \le \bar{R}(j) \qquad \text{for } j = 1, \ldots, \bar{j}.$$

The set of constraints in Equation (4.1) reflects resource availability. It states the total extraction of copper from resources of each grade, projected for the period covered by the model, cannot exceed total amount of copper available in that grade.

Delivery of Resources

(4.5) $$\sum_{m=1}^{\bar{m}} C(m,n) \le \sum_{j=1}^{\bar{j}} X(j,n) + \sum_{q=1}^{\bar{q}} Y(q,n) \qquad \text{for } n = 1, \ldots, \bar{n}.$$

Equation (4.5) specifies the materials balance in the copper industry. For each period n, total deliveries of copper to all users $\Sigma C(m,n)$, can be no greater than total extraction, $\Sigma X(j,n)$, plus total recycling during that period, $\Sigma Y(q,n)$.

Capital Stock

(4.6) $$U(m,n) = \sum_{r=0}^{2}\left[C(m,n-r) + \sum_{k=1}^{\bar{k}} \frac{A(k,m,n-r)}{\bar{E}(k,m)} \right]$$

$$\text{for } m = 1, \ldots, \bar{m}; n = 3, \ldots, \bar{n}.$$

The constraints in Equation (4.6) concern the capital stock held by copper users. The copper-equivalent capital stock in use, denoted $U(m,n)$, is the stock of copper embedded in the equipment in use by demand category m in period n, plus the analogous copper-equivalent in the stock of substitutes. The latter is calculated by division of the quantity of the substitute $A(k,m,n-r)$ by the conversion factor $\bar{E}(k,m)$. Assuming three-period (thirty-year) lifetimes of the capital goods in which the copper or its substitute is embedded, the stock in this example is total deliveries in the current and the two preceding ten-year periods.

Demand

(4.7) $U(m,n) = D(m,n) \geq \bar{D}(m,n)$

for $m = 1, \ldots, \bar{m}; n = 1, \ldots, \bar{n}$.

The constraints in Equation (4.7) ensure that the copper program meets the demand requirements. The first equality states that the total amount of copper services provided $[D(m,n)]$ is (through appropriate definition of units) equal to the copper-equivalent capital stock in use $[U(m,n)]$. The second part of the equation, the inequality, ensures that the total quantity of copper services provided, $D(m,n)$, is no less than the exogenously given requirements path, $\bar{D}(m,n)$. The actual demand requirements in $\bar{D}$ are exogenous, specified along lines discussed in Chapter 3.

Recycling

(4.8) $S(q,n) = S(q,n-1) - Y(q,n) + \sum_{m=1}^{\bar{m}} [\bar{F}(q,m)C(m,n-3)]$

for $q = 1, \ldots, \bar{q}; n = 4, \ldots, \bar{n}$.

We divide scrapped copper into several recycling categories. This final constraint states that $S(q,n)$, the total stock of scrapped copper in each recycling category q at the end of period n, is equal to carryover from the preceding period, $S(q,n-1)$, plus the amount scrapped in period n, $\Sigma F(q,m)C(m,n-3)$, minus the amount actually recycled, $Y(q,n)$.

Initial Conditions

Because most of the above constraints relate each period to previous periods, they have a slightly different form for the first three periods. ($n = 1,2,3$). The changes can be seen by inspection of each equation or inequality. Constraints in (4.4) have an initial extraction constraint to reflect the assumption that mining commitments last 20 years. Constraints in (4.6) include estimates of copper-equivalent capital in place at the beginning of the first period. Finally, the recycling constraints in (4.8) reflect estimates of initial stocks of scrap plus scrappage from copper capital in periods before the first.

5 Findings of the Copper Model

We now present the results of the copper model: the outputs of the linear-programming (LP) problem of which the geologic, substitution, recycling, and demand data are the inputs. First we unfold the "base case," our best guess as to the parameters of the copper-exhaustion model. Next we present the results of a number of sensitivity analyses in which we vary those uncertain parameters we think most important. Then we investigate the impact of technological advance on patterns of resource exhaustion. Finally, we offer an estimate of the macroeconomic significance of copper scarcity.

The Base Case

Table 5.1 presents a brief overview of the assumptions of the model that follows. We discuss the base case with respect to the projected allocation and production patterns, the time paths for recycling and substitution, and the time paths for the efficiency prices. We reiterate at this point that of all the assumptions, the one most likely to prove inaccurate is the assumption of no future inventions and innovations. Because of the importance of this assumption, we will return to the topic toward the end of this chapter.

We emphasize that the numbers below should be viewed with appropriate caution. They are not forecasts of the course of events in the copper industry over the next century; rather, they are *conditional projections* of a set of price and quantity paths. By "conditional" we mean that they depend in a crucial way on the inputs we have entered into our model. Moreover, as we shall see in the next section, in many cases the numbers tend to be sensitive to our assumptions. The major issue we shall confront, however, is the extent to which copper scarcity is in an economic sense "large" or "small." Is the finiteness of our copper resources likely to be inconsequential for economic growth and future living standards, or are we about to enter a "new Iron Age" with the drastic implications for our style of life that such reentry might entail?

Table 5.1   Assumptions for base case of copper model

Structure of the model
  The analysis relies on a linear-programming model. It minimizes the dis-
    counted costs of meeting a predetermined trajectory of copper-equivalent
    services, subject to technological constraints.
Assumptions
  Resources: 22 cost categories of copper, including 1 superabundant "back-
    stop" resource available at very high cost.
  Demand: 21 demand categories. Each grows exogenously, proportional to
    total output.
  Substitution: Alternative materials considered are aluminum, titanium, plastic,
    stainless steel, carbon steel, and glass optical fiber. Each is assumed to be
    superabundant at constant cost.
  Planning horizon: 180 years, or 18 ten-year periods.
  Growth rate of GNP: 3 percent per annum from 1970 to 2070, and 1 percent
    per annum thereafter.
  Discount rate: 8 percent per annum through 2070 and 4 percent per annum
    thereafter (discount rate is corrected for inflation).

Allocation Patterns

Mining. In Chapters 1 and 2 we discussed the availability of copper resources-in-the-ground. A key problem addressed by our study is the *efficient* pattern of resource extraction and exhaustion, that is, the pattern that
minimizes the economic costs expressed in the objective function described in Chapter 4. Figure 5.1 illustrates the computed pattern of efficient
extraction of copper ores. More complete data are provided in the Appendix at the end of this chapter, Tables 5A.1 to 5A.9. (Note that in this
chapter "ton" refers to the metric ton.) The extraction curve shows that
the rate of extraction increases over the next century and that the backstop
ores[1] come into use in the tenth decade. When backstop ores are required,
copper will be extremely expensive—around $130 per kilogram by our
reckoning—but superabundant. At that point the problem of resource scarcity disappears for copper.

  Substitution. One of the major innovations in the current study is its use
of engineering data on the cost of substitution to provide estimates of a
demand curve for a product or service. The calculated efficient pattern of
substitution away from copper is shown in Appendix Table 5A.2 for the
base case. Figure 5.2 illustrates the takeover paths for a number of the

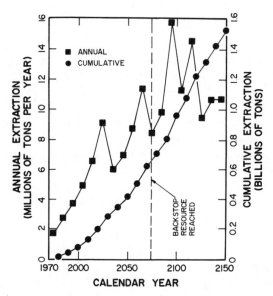

Figure 5.1 The annual and cumulative extraction of copper metal computed for the base case. (Throughout Chapter 5 "tons" are metric tons.) After the year 2075 all copper ores are exhausted and copper metal is extracted only from rock, the backstop resource. (Based on data from Appendix Table 5A.1.)

individual categories. The base case model predicts that substitution will occur at different points for three broad groups—now, later, or never. The early group—where substitution is generally already under way—includes eight categories, such as car radiators, power wire, transformers, and building pipe. Our calculations show that copper will no longer be used in products in these categories after the end of the twentieth century. There is also a group of applications for which there are no cheap substitutes for copper, and the model predicts that copper will serve in these uses for 150 years or more. They include several uses in communications, very small and very large electric motors, industrial heat exchangers, and electronic wire.

The model also predicts a shift in the sectors where copper is used. In the late 1960s, according to data reported in Table 3.4, a large quantity of copper was devoted to established technology. For example, 83 percent of the copper stock was in copper wiring and pipe in homes and in electrical transmission lines. By the end of the study period, most of the copper in use will serve in electronic or communications categories.[2]

Recycling. The model also predicts the pattern of efficient recycling of copper in the future. Because the cost of recycling increases as the fraction of metal recycled in each recycling category increases, we expect to see the fraction of copper recycled rise over time as the real price of copper increases. Figure 5.3 and Appendix Table 5A.3 show the recycling pattern from each category as a fraction of total copper deliveries. The top line of Figure 5.3 shows that the share of total copper deliveries met by recycling moves up from around 30 percent in early periods to around 70 percent by

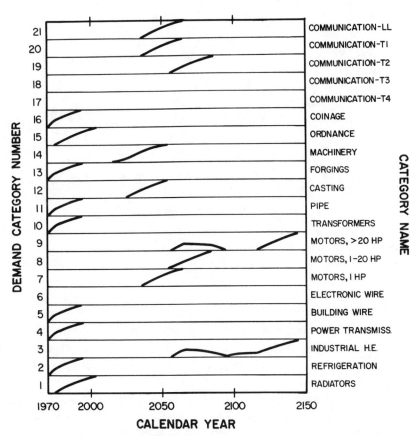

Figure 5.2 The pattern of substitution in the different demand categories computed for the base case. The panels show the fraction of demand in each category met through use of substitutes. The bottom panel, for example, shows that aluminum, the substitute material for copper in radiators, is not used until 1970 but takes over the entire market by the end of the decade 2000–2009. Note that the sizes of the demand categories vary widely, as shown in Table 5.2. (Based on data from Appendix Table 5A.3.)

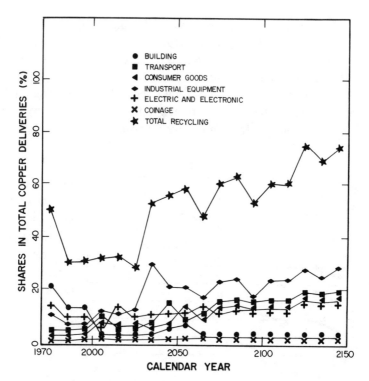

Figure 5.3 The contribution from each category of scrap to deliveries of copper metal calculated for the base case. Recycling meets 30 percent of the demand for copper in the early decades but 70 percent in the last decade. (Based on data from Appendix Table 5A.3.)

the end of our time horizon. The reason for this increase is that "mining" copper from scrap is cheaper than mining copper from the extremely low grade backstop ores that will be the only source of new copper by the end of the next century.

Figure 5.4 and Table 5A.4 show the predicted stocks of unrecycled copper and the annual rate of recycling. The total amount of recycling rises over time from an amount on the order of 1–2 million tons per year in early periods to around 25 million tons annually at the end. In early periods, up to the middle of the next century, stocks available for recycling increase as old capital equipment is scrapped and allowed to lie fallow. The model predicts that it will become progressively cheaper to mine old scrapheaps than new low-grade ores by the middle of the next century, after which the stocks of scrap will be used up very rapidly.[3]

The demand for copper. Table 5.2 lists the estimated demand and substitution costs for the major demand categories in 1970–1979. The last column shows for each category the calculated switch price, the price of copper metal at which the cost of using the copper-based technology exactly equals the cost of using the substitute technology.

One of the standard tools of economics is the demand curve which relates the quantity of a good purchased to its price, other things being held equal. In the conventional economic approach, a demand curve is derived from estimates based on price and quantity data. In the materials-modeling approach, the underlying demand functions are derived from substitution, technological, or cost data, as described in Chapter 3.

To illustrate the way we calculate the demand for copper, we show in Figure 5.5 an *engineering demand function.* This curve illustrates the relation between the price of copper and the percent of the demand for copper-

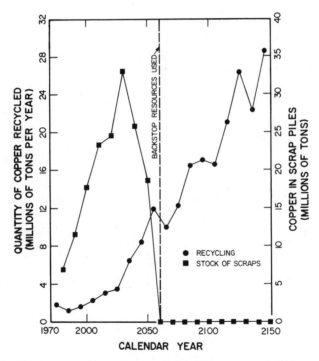

Figure 5.4   The amount of copper recycled and the amount held in scrap piles in the base case. By the time that copper ores are exhausted, all copper scrap is recycled and the accumulated stocks of scrap are gone. (Based on data from Appendix Table 5A.4.)

Table 5.2 Demand and substitution costs in 1970–1979

Demand category	Demand[a] (thousand tons per decade)	Share in total demand (%)	Substitute material	Switch point ($ per kg copper)[b]
1. Radiators	1,506	4.04	Aluminum	2.10
2. Refrigeration	2,427	6.52	Aluminum	0.73
3. Industrial heat exchangers	415	1.11	Titanium	93.4
4. Power transmission cable	5,860	15.73	Aluminum	0.0
5. Building wire	11,767	31.59	Aluminum	0.0
6. Electronic wire	3,398	9.12	Aluminum	184
7. Motors, <1 HP	4	0.01	Aluminum	21.0
8. Motors, 1–20 HP	263	0.71	Aluminum	72.3
9. Motors, >20 HP	373	1.00	Aluminum	98.7
10. Transformers	440	1.18	Aluminum	1.50
11. Pipe	6,781	18.21	Plastic	1.56
12. Castings	1,404	3.77	Stainless steel	11.7
13. Forgings	477	1.28	Stainless steel	1.08
14. Machinery	546	1.47	Stainless steel	7.25
15. Ordnance	53	0.14	Carbon steel	2.51
16. Coinage	1,144	3.07	Zinc	1.49
17. Communication T4	0.04	0.00	Fiber	668.0
18. Communication T3	0.4	0.00	Fiber	372.0
19. Communication T2	1	0.00	Fiber	67.0
20. Communication T1	10	0.03	Fiber	22.5
21. Communication LL	379	1.02	Fiber	20.0
Total	37,247	100.0		

a. Demand for copper or copper-equivalent services, estimated for first time period (1970–1979).
b. All costs are in U.S. dollars, 1978 prices.

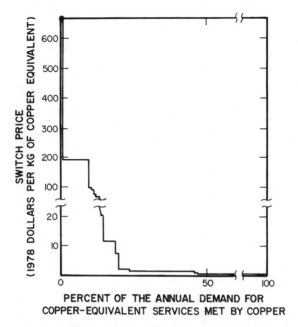

Figure 5.5   The engineering demand function for copper for the decade 1970–1979. This function shows the percentage of the annual demand for copper-equivalent services met by copper as a function of the switch price, the price at which demand is met by use of an alternative material. The switch price is expressed in 1978 dollars per kilogram of copper-equivalent material.

equivalent services that is met by copper. As the price of copper rises, a larger and larger fraction of copper uses hit their switch prices and convert to substitute materials, with the demand for copper itself therefore declining as substitutes gain a larger share of the market for copper-equivalent services.

Total material balances in copper services. A useful way of summarizing the flows of the demand and supply of copper is to examine the *material balances,* or total flows of copper metal. These are represented in Figures 5.6 and 5.7, which illustrate one of the most important results of our study. The demand for copper services grows rapidly, but in the future a larger and larger fraction of the demand will be met by copper substitutes. We estimate that by the end of the next century more than 90 percent of the services now provided by copper will be met by the use of substitute materials, such as aluminum.[4] Put differently, even though the demand for

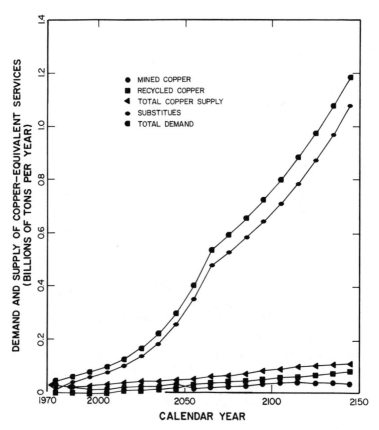

Figure 5.6   The total demand for copper computed in the base case (upper curve) and the amounts supplied by new copper, recycled copper, and substitute materials. (Based on data from Appendix Table 5A.5.)

copper-equivalent services is estimated to rise by a factor of 32, mining is estimated to rise by a factor of only six.

Prices

Before we discuss the pattern of price movements in the efficient program, a few introductory words are in order. A fundamental economic question is how to utilize exhaustible resources effectively over time. The stock of resources consists of a continuum, moving from high-grade and low-cost ores (such as the open-pit deposits of copper in Arizona and Utah) to low-grade and high-cost sources (such as the backstop resources that contain no copper minerals). Our LP model computes a set of efficiency prices that correspond to the efficient allocation of copper-equivalent services. These efficiency prices are the signals that tell producers and consumers about the relative scarcity of different goods. (A more detailed discussion of efficiency prices appeared in Chapter 1.) We can provide three different but equivalent interpretations of the efficiency prices presented in this section.

1. The technical explanation of the efficiency prices (sometimes called shadow prices or dual variables) is that they tell us how much the objective function (total discounted costs of providing copper-equivalent services) will change when a variable changes by one unit. For example, the efficiency prices of unmined copper tell us how much the economy would benefit in terms of lower discounted production costs if there were one extra unit of copper metal in a given grade.

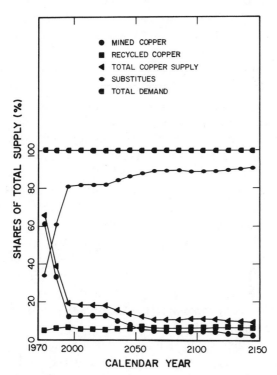

Figure 5.7 The proportions of the total demand for copper supplied by new copper, recycled copper, and substitute materials as computed for the base case. (Based on data from Appendix Table 5A.5.)

2. A second view interprets efficiency prices in terms of an ideal centrally planned economy. A central planner, charged with attaining an efficient allocation of copper resources over time, would set prices to consumers and producers that were equal to the efficiency prices. The efficiency prices of copper ores, for example, would show how much unmined copper should be extracted.

3. Finally, and most important, the efficiency prices correspond to the outcomes of a perfectly competitive market. A competitive market faced with exactly the same conditions as we have found (for geology, substitution, demand and so on) would grind out exactly the same prices as the efficiency prices we have computed. We have called this the correspondence principle between markets and LP (see Chapter 1).

Having noted these three interpretations of the efficiency prices that we are about to present, we must emphasize the tentative character of the results. They are conditional projections; they depend entirely on the structure of the model and the data we have put into it and represent no more than the results of an imperfect and uncertain mechanism for foretelling future patterns of economic activity.

Before going into a detailed discussion of prices, we must recall different price concepts. In our LP model and solution, as in the real world, different price concepts apply at different points. The two most important are these.

1. The *royalty* or *scarcity rent* on unmined copper, or copper-in-the-ground, is the efficiency price of copper before any extraction has occurred. In the United States today, this royalty is contained in the value of mineral rights attached to a given parcel of land. In the LP model, we examine the concept of the "intrinsic scarcity" of unmined copper; this concept signifies the efficiency price of unmined copper.

2. The *market price of copper metal* is the value that smelted and refined copper metal commands. In the real world, it corresponds to the price that applies to ordering a bar of copper from a local wholesaler or to the copper prices quoted in the financial pages of the newspaper. The copper model also calculates the efficiency price on delivered copper metal. Moreover, the market price of copper metal equals the royalty plus the cost of mining, beneficiation, refining, and transportation that occurs before the metal reaches the wholesaler or the London Metals Exchange.

Scarcity rents on copper. In a competitive market or an efficient program, a royalty or scarcity rent will be associated with each scarce natural resource. For example, a deposit of copper that is much less costly to mine than is the bulk of other deposits will command a scarcity rent that reflects the lower relative extraction cost.

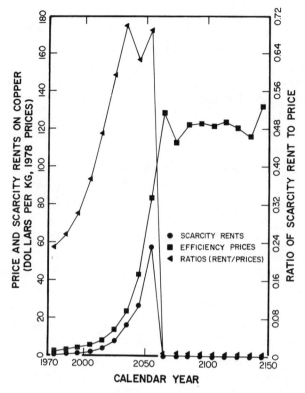

Figure 5.8 The scarcity rents, efficiency prices, and their ratio as computed for the base case. Prices are expressed as 1978 dollars per kilogram.

In our model, the most important scarcity rents arise on scarce, unmined copper. Figure 5.8 shows the scarcity rents on the lowest grade of copper mined during each period as projected by the model. For each individual deposit, the royalty rises over time at a rate equal to the market interest rate until the deposit is exhausted.

Such patterns are seen in the scarcity rents shown in Table 5A.7 in the Appendix. The scarcity rents in the first period fall off sharply from the low-cost to the high-cost copper deposits. Moreover, there is *a zero scarcity rent* on the high-cost but superabundant backstop deposits, as predicted by economic theory. This zero scarcity rent signifies that, once higher-grade resources have been exhausted and the price of copper has become high enough to cover the cost of mining the backstop resource, copper ore is no longer intrinsically scarce because the backstop is an inexhaustible resource.

Figure 5.8 shows the relative importance of the scarcity rent to the market price of copper metal. The scarcity rent starts out at a low level in the first few decades, then rises sharply as the economy moves to high-cost but still scarce ores. Finally, as the backstop ores are being depleted at the end of the period, the scarcity rents disappear. Thus the ratio of scarcity rent to market price rises from around one-quarter to three-quarters, then falls to zero. The remainder (in 1970–1979, for example, 73 percent of the market price) is the share of the price accounted for by the capital and labor costs required to extract and refine the ore to produce copper metal.

The large ratio of scarcity rent to price shows the importance of considering resource scarcity in planning for efficient allocation of copper resources. If this factor were ignored, copper would be very significantly underpriced in markets.

The price of copper. The next important question in the efficient program concerns the efficiency price of copper metal from now until the time of exhaustion of copper ores. As can be seen in Table 5.3 and Figure 5.8, we project that the efficiency price of copper metal will rise very steeply over the next century. Starting from an original efficiency price of $2.44 per kilogram in the decade 1970–1979 (in 1978 prices), the price of copper metal is estimated to rise to about $120 per kilogram at the end of the twenty-first century. The price increase is rapid and continuous over the first ten decades of our estimation period, averaging about 4 percent per annum through 2070. During this period the total increase reaches a factor of 50. The rise stops when the scarce copper ores have been exhausted and when the backstop resources start to be mined.

What is the relationship between our calculated efficiency price and the market price? If the model and the data were perfectly accurate, we would expect the efficiency price in recent years to correspond to the actual market price. Table 5.4 compares our estimate of the efficiency price of copper metal with the actual figures for recent years. The price forecast in our model is higher than the actual average price of copper for the 1970s and early 1980s. However, given the highly structural nature of the model, as well as uncertainties discussed later in this chapter and in Chapter 6, we are satisfied that the comparisons of actual and efficiency prices are as close as could reasonably be expected.

Overall, the forecast for the scarcity of copper might at first blush appear alarming. Copper's efficiency price is estimated to rise nearly as high as today's prices for rare metals (like silver at its peak). If *today's* copper deliveries in the United States were to be met at the estimated backstop

Table 5.3   Efficiency price of copper

Period	Decade	Calculated efficiency price ($ per kg)	Average increase in 10 years (% per annum)	Average increase in 50 years (% per annum)
1	1970–1979	2.44	—	
2	1980–1989	3.17	2.65	
3	1990–1999	4.27	3.02	3.51
4	2000–2009	5.93	3.35	
5	2010–2019	8.71	3.92	
6	2020–2029	13.69	4.62	
7	2030–2039	23.40	5.51	
8	2040–2049	42.53	6.16	
9	2050–2059	83.46	6.97	4.31
10	2060–2069	128.44	4.40	
11	2070–2079	112.72	−1.30	
12	2080–2089	121.76	0.77	
13	2090–2099	122.61	0.07	
14	2100–2109	121.36	−0.10	0.13
15	2110–2119	123.21	0.15	
16	2120–2129	120.47	−0.22	
17	2130–2139	115.39	−0.43	
18	2140–2149	132.04	1.36	

Source: Base case run for copper. Prices are in 1978 dollars.

Table 5.4   Actual and efficiency prices of copper metal (1978 dollars per kg copper)

Decade	Actual price	Efficiency price
1960–1969	1.55	Not available
1970–1979	1.68	2.44
1980–1984	1.28	2.96

price of $125 per kilogram, the cost of producing today's national output would increase by around 2 percent.[5] But, of course, the economy of the twenty-first century will not use the same amount of copper per unit of output as is used today. We calculate that by the time copper prices have risen from $2 to $120 per kilogram at the end of our projection period, the amount of copper in use will have fallen from 0.15 kilogram to 0.02 kilogram per dollar of output—a drop of 1.2 percent per annum in the copper-intensity of output. To obtain the true impact of the scarcity of copper resources on economic welfare, therefore, we must examine the actual prices of copper services.

The price of copper-equivalent services. As substitution of other materials for copper occurs, the price of final copper-equivalent services ("price of services" for short) will not rise as steeply as the price of copper metal. For example, even though the price of copper doubles, the cost of materials in automobile radiators will go up by much less as aluminum is substituted for copper in radiators. A key issue for this study, then, concerns the movement of the ultimate price of services.

Appendix Table 5A.8 shows the movement of the price of services over our estimation period for each component of copper demand. Table 5.5 lists the prices for the ten largest sectors (where the values for 1970–1979 are set equal to 100) and also calculates three different kinds of price indexes for copper services:

1. The *quantity-weighted index* I_1 is the average price for copper-equivalent services weighted by the 1975 share of consumption of copper in each sector.

2. The *value-weighted index* I_2 weighs the prices by the value of copper-equivalent services. This second index, more meaningful economically than I_1, corresponds to the customary fixed-weight index used to construct items like the Consumer Price Index.

3. It is well-known that fixed-weight price indexes tend to overstate the cost-of-living increase from changing prices because they do not allow for consumers to substitute low-cost for high-cost commodities. To correct for this bias we calculate the *geometric index* I_3. This index calculates the geometric mean of the prices of copper-equivalent services, using as weights the shares of 1975 values for copper-equivalent services.[6]

Our estimates for these indexes appear graphically in Figure 5.9. For the span from period 1 to period 14 (that is, through the period 2100–2109) we obtain the estimated average rate of increase of prices shown in Table 5.6. The price of services shows a markedly smaller rise than does the price of copper metal. If no substitution were to occur, the price index of copper goods would rise by a factor of 50 over the 130 years. But with substitution of alternative materials, it rises only by a factor of from 2.3 to 7.1, depending on the price index used. The difference in behavior of the metal price and the service price is a vivid illustration of how substitution can alleviate materials exhaustion.

Table 5.5 Prices for copper-equivalent services in ten largest demand sectors and indexes for all services

Demand category	Substitute material	1970–1979	1980–1989	1990–1999	2000–2009	2010–2019	2020–2029	2030–2039	2040–2049	2050–2059	2060–2069	2070–2079	2080–2089	2090–2099
Radiators (1)	Aluminum	100[a]	100	100	100	100	101	98	101	109	76	76	87	71
Refrigeration (2)	Aluminum	100	100	100	100	100	101	98	101	109	76	76	87	71
Power transmission (4)	Aluminum	100	100	100	100	100	100	100	100	100	100	100	100	100
Building wire (5)	Aluminum	100	100	100	100	100	100	100	100	100	100	100	100	100
Electronic wire (6)	Aluminum	100	122	158	199	243	337	467	480	2,437	5,059	3,041	4,022	3,935
Pipe (11)	Plastic	100	100	100	100	100	101	98	101	109	76	76	87	71
Castings (12)	Stainless steel	100	122	146	212	256	229	609	631	677	477	477	544	444
Forging (13)	Stainless steel	100	100	100	100	100	101	98	101	109	76	76	87	71
Machinery (14)	Stainless steel	100	122	165	193	237	398	385	399	428	301	301	344	281
Coinage (16)	Zinc	100	100	100	100	100	101	98	101	109	76	76	87	71
Average final price														
Arithmetic average														
Volume (I_1)[b]		100	104	110	118	127	140	168	181	431	689	470	594	558
Value (I_2)[c]		100	106	114	126	138	156	196	213	565	933	623	797	748
Geometric Average														
Value (I_3)[d]		100	105	112	119	126	134	147	153	210	183	204	185	182

a. Prices set at 100 for 1970–1979.
b. Prices of copper-equivalent services weighted by use of copper metal in 1975.
c. Prices of copper-equivalent services weighted by the value of copper-equivalent services in 1975.
d. Geometric mean of copper-equivalent prices using 1975 value weights.

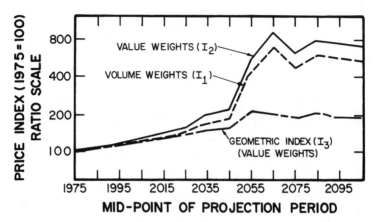

Figure 5.9 Price index for copper-equivalent services (on a ratio scale with the price in 1975 set at 100) computed for the base case. "Volume weights" weigh the price of services by the volumes of copper consumption in 1970; "value weights" weigh the product of the volumes in 1970 times the efficiency prices of copper-equivalent services. The geometric index is computed using 1970 value weights.

Table 5.6 Calculated price increases for copper metal and copper services, from 1970–1979 to 2100–2109

Item	Average increase (% per annum)
Copper price	3.1
Price of copper services	
Arithmetic average	
Quantity weights	1.3
Value weights	1.5
Geometric average	
Value weights	0.92

The value of copper stockpiles. Finally, consider the value of copper in junkheaps—scrapped copper before it is recycled. The principles of valuation of junkheaps are similar to those of valuation of unmined copper, except the scrap is produced as a by-product of old production.

The valuation of copper junk is essentially forward-looking. If no pieces of scrap will ever be recycled, it will always have zero value (technically, it will always have a zero efficiency price). That a piece of copper junk will be recycled at some point in the future gives it value today. Moreover, during the period of waiting to be recycled, the efficiency price of the junk must rise at the interest rate. For example, say that a discarded machine is currently not recycled but that it will be recycled in 20 years, at which time the copper in it (after costs of recycling) will be worth $30 per kilogram. For anyone to want to hold the scrap, at an 8 percent discount rate, it must be worth $30 \times 1.08^{-20} = \$6.44$ today.

Figure 5.10 and Appendix Table 5A.9 illustrate the efficiency price of copper scrap in the different recycling categories. The efficiency price of copper scrap rises considerably over the period under consideration. For example, copper in the highest "grade" of scrap, the scrap from buildings (pipe and electric wire), rises in value from $2.29 per kilogram in 1970–1979 to $121 per kilogram in 2080–2089.

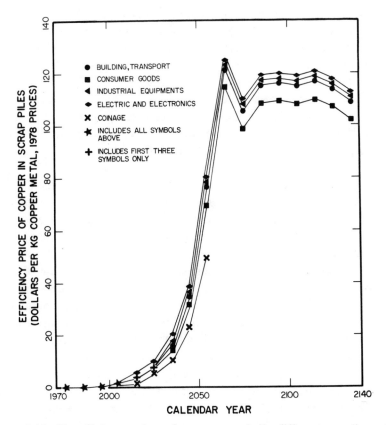

Figure 5.10   The efficiency prices of scrap copper in the different recycling categories (in 1978 dollars per kilogram) computed for the base case.

Table 5.7   Estimated value of copper scrap, 1975

Category of scrap	Value of best unrecycled scrap[a] (cents per kg, 1978 prices)
Building	16
Transport	16
Consumer goods	15
Industrial equipment	18
Electric	24

a. The best unrecycled scrap is the highest-valued scrap that is not recycled in the first period.

It is also of interest to ask how valuable is the copper that lies in scrap but has not yet been recycled. Such calculations would be useful for recycling policy in the event the private markets were unwilling to store potentially valuable scrap containing copper. Table 5.7 shows our estimate of the efficiency value of the best unused copper scrap by recycling category as of 1980 (these represent the values of the metal *before* any costs of extraction from the scrapheaps). The value of unrecycled scrap appears to be in the range of 15–25 cents per kilogram, quite low relative to the estimated efficiency price of copper metal ($2.44 per kilogram).

The base case presents a classic example of resource exhaustion over time. The efficiency price of copper in the different program rises steadily over the coming decades. As it rises, the cost of obtaining the services now performed by copper rises on every front: lower-grade ores are mined, the fraction of copper recycled increases, and substitute high-cost materials gradually invade the realm of copper use. When the exhaustion of high-grade copper resources occurs—around 2150 by our reckoning—the mining of copper will be much smaller relative to the size of the economy than it is today, and the amount of substitution will be large. Aluminum and other substitutes will take over nearly all the services provided by copper. By the backstop era at the end of the next century, copper metal and many copper services will be quite expensive by today's standards; but at the then prevailing elevated prices, resource exhaustion will no longer curb growth because the high-cost copper and substitute materials will be superabundant.

Sensitivity Analysis for Specific Uncertainties

The results just reported represent our best guess as to the efficient use of copper resources over time. But any projection so far into the future raises uncertainties about many of the major assumptions used in the model. How much copper will be discovered? Will aluminum provide a viable substitute for all those services in which we have designated it the best alternative material? Will environmental constraints on mining backstop resources prove an insuperable obstacle to further copper mining once the high-grade ores have been exhausted? And, perhaps most important, what hand will be dealt by future technological developments? Will new products and processes generate new uses for copper that increase demands? Will innovations emerge to meet the demand for copper? Or, perhaps, will scientists find miraculous new materials that mimic entirely the key properties of copper at low costs? These uncertainties are among the many hazards for analysts who venture toward a quantitative assessment of the future.

In making conditional projections, we would very much like to present some kind of confidence bounds around our estimates. There are no theoretical obstacles to using the formal structure of modern decision theory to determine these bounds. For example, in a similar model Nordhaus and Yohe (1983) estimated the error bounds in a long-run energy–carbon dioxide model in which there were ten important unknown parameters. In the present case, however, that approach is beyond our capabilities. It would first require putting error bounds upon the hundred or so important parameters of the model. We would then have to make on the order of ten thousand model runs in order to calculate the directional derivatives of the output variables with respect to the input assumptions. This research project could clearly exhaust both patience and budgets.

The sensitivity analysis used here is an alternative approach. This technique explores the results of changing key parameters in the model; the changes in the parameters were chosen intuitively rather than systematically, but we have attempted to impose some discipline on the process by explicitly determining the degree of likelihood attached to the alternative scenarios or events. In what follows we have chosen alternative numerical values for our sensitivity parameters by examining changes that represent moderately likely occurrences, those that have, say, between 1 in 4 and 1 in 10 chances of occurring. We first list the set of sensitivity runs, then discuss the effects of changing these key variables.

The Cases

Time truncation. In principle, allocation of scarce resources takes place over infinite time. Truncation of the time period may result in an undervaluing of resources because none have been conserved for the future. On the other hand, if the program runs until backstop resources are mined, then truncation should have no effect.

To test the effect of truncation we chose one shorter period, run 01 (100 years), and one longer, run 02 (250 years).

Case 1A (run 01)   Short time truncation of 100 years.

Case 1B (run 02)   Long time truncation of 250 years.

Economic growth. For our base-case run we assumed that the GNP will grow at a robust rate, 3 percent annually, until the end of the "growth epoch" in 2070, and will slow down to 1 percent growth per annum after that point. Because we also assumed the demand for copper-equivalent services would grow at those rates, changing the length of the growth epoch has a marked effect on demand for copper-equivalent services. We therefore tested (in run 03) for the effect of slow economic growth (where the period of rapid growth lasts only 50 years) and rapid economic growth (in run 04, where rapid growth lasts for 150 years).

Case 2A (run 03)   Slow economic growth.

Case 2B (run 04)   Rapid economic growth.

Changes in geological availability of copper. One of the major uncertainties of the model revolves around the amount of copper resources that will be available and their cost. To test for sensitivity we performed a number of different runs, as follows:

Case 3A (run 05)   In this run we assumed that there were no backstop copper resources, perhaps because of environmental constraints. This case (as well as case 3B) is a particularly important one, because the amount of mining of rock (as opposed to metal) required in the use of the backstop resources is astronomical by today's standards. If society thought it unacceptable to mine such large volumes of rock or imposed heavy costs on reclaiming the land, then the cost of using the backstop technology would be much higher.

Case 3B (run 06)   As a variant on 3A, we quadrupled the cost of the backstop resources.

Case 3C (run 07)   Conversely, since the backstop resources may be much cheaper than expected, in this sensitivity run we reduced the cost of backstop ores by 75 percent.

Case 3D (run 13)   All extraction costs were doubled.

Case 3E (run 18)   The resource base was decreased by 50 percent in all grades.

Case 3F (run 17)   The resource base was increased by 50 percent in all grades.

Alternative recycling technologies. One of the least satisfactory aspects of the data base was our estimate of the recycling costs. In this area, then, our sensitivity runs reflect this uncertainty about costs.

Case 4A (run 10)   All recycling costs were halved.

Case 4B (run 12)   All recycling costs were doubled.

We also determined the exhaustion patterns that would result if *no* recycling occurred.

Case 4C (run 11)   All recycling activities were eliminated.

Substitution. Given the complexity of the substitution model, we could perform but a limited number of sensitivity runs for substitution costs.

Case 5A (run 19)   We first estimated the impact of doubling *all* substitution costs.

Case 5B (run 20)   All substitution costs were halved.

We then did sensitivity analyses on those demand categories in which the uncertainties were particularly high.

Case 5C (run 15)   The cost of substitution for copper in electronic wire was decreased to $10 per kilogram of copper-equivalent from the $380 per kilogram cost of the base case.

Case 5D (run 16)   The costs of substitution were increased for building wire by $8 per kilogram copper, for heat ex-
changers by $82 per kilogram copper, and for
transformers by $1 per kilogram copper.

Discount rate. The discount rate is an important component of the efficiency prices of scarce resources.

Case 6A (run 08)   The discount rate was increased by 2 percent per
annum.

Case 6B (run 09)   The discount rate was decreased by 2 percent per
annum.

Unfavorable outcomes. Often luck comes in winning or losing streaks.
To evaluate the outcome of a number of unfavorable circumstances that
might occur, we took combinations of the above events.

Case 7A (run 24)   Pessimistic run. We assumed that copper extraction was limited (as in cases 3B, 3D, and 3E), substitution more expensive (case 5A), and recycling
costs doubled (case 4B).

Case 7B (run 25)   Very pessimistic run. We made the same assumptions as in case 7A, plus more rapid demand for
copper due to high economic growth per case 2B.

Favorable outcomes. A symmetrical set of favorable outcomes was also
considered.

Case 8A (run 26)   Optimistic case. We assumed mining costs were
low (run 3C), recycling costs were low (run 4A),
substitution was easy (run 5B), and resources were
abundant (run 3F).

In addition, we combined these with slow growth of copper demand.

Case 8B (run 27)   Very optimistic run. We made the same assumptions as in 8A, plus slow growth in demand per
case 2A.

Copper availability. We ran a sensitivity analysis (run 21) to calculate
how resource allocation and prices would differ if copper were superabundant at a price approximately equal to the price of copper today (the cost of
using resource grade 1). This is equivalent to assuming that a new process

is discovered for producing unlimited amounts of copper at today's costs, or that a new material is synthesized that mimics all the properties of copper at low cost.

Case 9 (run 21)   Remove copper scarcity.

Case 10   Copper disappears.

The Results

To present all the results for all the variables for all the sensitivity analyses would be cruel (if not unusual) punishment. We present instead the highlights, suggesting where the results are quite sensitive and where they are not. Several runs were eliminated at the outset. We were not surprised to learn that time truncation made no significant difference until the end of the period under study. More surprising was the finding that doubling or halving recycling costs made no major impact on any variable (except the quantity recycled). These sensitivity runs are thus omitted.

Extraction. We begin with the effect of the different assumptions on the rate of extraction of copper and on the cumulative amount of copper extracted. Table 5.8 shows the first-period and eleventh-period rates of extraction, as well as the cumulative extraction, for each of our nontrivial cases.

Only modest differences in the extraction of copper at the beginning of the study period arise in most of the sensitivity runs. The largest effect is caused by increasing the substitution costs and by counterfactually eliminating all recycling. Surprisingly, the cumulative extraction over the first 110 years of the study period remains quite stable across the wide set of extreme assumptions we have included. Cumulative copper extraction ranges from around 300 million tons for the pessimistic case of 1,110 million tons for the case in which recycling is eliminated. This robustness arises because copper is limited by supply over the period. There are, however, quite marked differences in cumulative extraction by the end of our 180-year span. In scenarios that admit the backstop technology of extracting copper from common rock, these differences begin to be large after 100 years or so. By the end of the 180-year period, for the optimistic case, the nation would have mined six times as much copper ore as in the pessimistic case.

Efficiency prices. Efficiency prices provide a fundamental index of the scarcity of copper, and we can use the prices found in the different sensitiv-

Table 5.8 Annual and cumulative extraction of copper in alternative cases (millions of tons, copper metal)

Run	Case	Description	Annual, 1970–1979	Annual, 2070–2079	Cumulative through 2079
0	00	Base case	1.7	8.4	703
		Alternative economic growth			
03	2A	Slow economic growth	1.7	1.7	412
04	2B	Rapid economic growth	1.7	16.2	765
		Discount rate			
08	6A	Increase by 2%	1.2	7.0	674
09	6B	Decrease by 2%	1.5	12.9	792
		Geology			
05	3A	No backstop ores	1.2	0	444
06	3B	Backstop cost × 4	1.7	1.7	534
07	3C	Backstop cost × 0.25	1.7	12.7	831
13	3D	Double extraction costs	1.1	0	534
18	3E	Resources × 0.5	1.2	11.3	673
17	3F	Resources × 1.5	1.8	7.6	802

11	4C	Eliminate recycling	2.9	16.6	1,110
		Substitution			
19	5A	Double substitution costs	4.0	16.7	867
20	5B	Halve substitution costs	1.2	0	534
15	5C	Decrease electronic wire substitution costs	1.7	3.2	443
16	5D	Increase miscellaneous substitution costs	6.3	13.0	794
24	7A	Pessimistic case	1.2	0	305
25	7B	Very pessimistic case	1.2	0	305
26	8A	Optimistic case	1.9	4.7	821
27	8B	Very optimistic case	1.9	3.5	516

ity runs as a way of gauging this intrinsic scarcity. If the price of copper is high, there are strong pressures for substitution, recycling, and the mining of low-grade ores; the opposite will be true when the price of copper is low.

Table 5.9 provides a summary of the results obtained for prices for the different runs. Columns (1) and (2) list the market price of copper (as it might be read in the *Wall Street Journal*) in 1975 and 2075. Examining first column (1), we see an astounding robustness of the copper price for 1975 across different runs, ranging from $1 to $6 per kilogram. Most of the cases lie between $2 and $4 per kilogram. It would take a most extraordinary conjunction of circumstances to convince us that the copper price should be far above or below today's level.

Column (2), on the other hand, shows wide variations across the different sets of assumptions in the predicted price of copper late in the next century. The range leaps from $6 per kilogram for the very optimistic case to $479 per kilogram for the pessimistic case. Why are the future prices so uncertain? One reason is that we know so little about future extraction costs of copper (compare runs 06 and 07, for example). This uncertainty may appear exaggerated, but we think it is not. If we had written this in 1800, what would we have predicted for the real price of copper? Would it have been surprising that the real price (in 1978 prices) would fall by 85 percent in the next 132 years? Would an observer thinking about energy in 1900 be surprised to learn that real electricity prices would fall by a factor of 30 by 1970, or that the real price of oil would quadruple from 1970 to 1980, or that oil prices would fall 60 percent from 1985 to 1986? The uncertainties that we have presented about future prices seem to us reasonable estimates of the intrinsic uncertainty an economy faces.

The last column of Table 5.9 shows the efficiency price of copper, or the scarcity rents or royalty on copper-in-the-ground. The efficiency price is the scarcity value of ores of the highest grade available in 1975. Put differently, it is what a nation should be willing to pay a magician who deposited some high-grade copper under the soil today.

The variation in the scarcity rent on unmined copper reflects the predicted variation in the computed 1975 market price of copper. The scarcity rent is estimated in the base case to be slightly under $1 per kilogram. For most nonextreme cases, the range of the scarcity rent lies between $0.70 and $2 per kilogram. Because it represents the value of copper before any mining or refining has taken place, the scarcity rent is the purest reflection of copper's intrinsic scarcity. By examining the last column in Table 5.9, we can get some idea of how scarce copper appears to be today (as valued in the model) and how this measure of intrinsic scarcity depends on different future conditions.

Technological Change

The single most important sensitivity run considers the possibility of future technological change in copper and related industries. In our discussion of this matter we rely on the following economic terminology. We denote as technological change those inventions, innovations, and advances in knowledge that expand society's range of practicable, productive processes. Technological change is to be distinguished from substitution, those changes in techniques actually employed among a given or existing set of technical possibilities. To see the difference, consider a society's technical possibilities at a point of time to be the book of all the available blueprints or recipes for combining different doses of land, labor, capital, and minerals into outputs. Technological change would represent the addition of new pages to the book of blueprints or recipes, say by invention of a new process. Substitution would, on the other hand, consist of selecting a different blueprint from among the available set for definite use in a given situation.

In actual practice it is impossible to measure technological change directly. The usual proxy for technological change is a measure of productivity, of which the most adequate is total factor productivity. Total factor productivity is calculated as the ratio of outputs to inputs, where outputs are measured as the market value of outputs in prices of a base year and inputs are a weighted average of inputs of labor, capital, and materials, the weights being proportional to a base year's market prices of inputs.

In the copper model we have up to now allowed for considerable substitution of different materials and processes for those based upon copper. We have not, however, allowed for the addition of brand-new or undiscovered processes or materials in the future and have thus ruled out future technological change. It must be noted that this distinction between substitution and technological change is somewhat artificial, for substitution to known but untested technologies often requires inventing new processes along the way. Although the boundary between substitution and technological change is in the real world blurred, we have nonetheless drawn the line by ruling out of our base case future materials or processes that are not within reach of current laboratory and engineering practices.

Table 5.9 Prices of copper in alternative runs (dollars per kg, 1978 prices)

Run	Case	Description	Market price of copper		Royalty or efficiency price of least expensive ores in 1975
			1975 (1)	2075 (2)	
0	00	Base case	2.44	113	0.93
		Alternative economic growth			
03	2A	Slow economic growth	2.41	33	0.89
04	2B	Rapid economic growth	2.45	140	0.94
		Discount rate			
08	6A	Increase by 2%	2.28	112	0.68
09	6B	Decrease by 2%	3.13	90	1.74
		Geology			
05	3A	No backstop ores	2.57	240	1.08
06	3B	Backstop cost × 4	2.53	240	1.03
07	3C	Backstop cost × 0.25	2.35	22	0.82
13	3D	Double extraction costs	4.67	240	1.68
18	3E	Resources × 0.5	3.60	121	1.98
17	3F	Resources × 1.5	2.24	91	0.70

11	4C	Eliminate recycling	3.30	120	1.68
		Substitution			
19	5A	Double substitution costs	3.53	85	1.68
20	5B	Halve substitution costs	2.35	119	0.86
15	5C	Decrease electronic wire substitution costs	2.31	18	0.79
16	5D	Increase miscellaneous substitution costs	3.73	84	1.86
24	7A	Pessimistic case	6.57	479	3.60
25	7B	Very pessimistic case	6.50	402	3.53
26	8A	Optimistic case	1.10	30	0.33
27	8B	Very optimistic case	1.09	6	0.32

As we have stressed above, we rule out technological change in the base case not because we believe it unlikely, but because we cannot accurately foresee future trends in innovation and fundamental invention. In this section, however, we speculate on the impact of technological change—tracing out the impact of hypothetical paths of cost reduction on the allocation of copper in the future.

To begin with, we should note that the base case will be consistent with technological change of a special variety—that known as "balanced" technological change. Technological change is said to be *balanced* when the reduction in the cost of production (or in the per unit cost of output) in each sector is just matched by the price increases of the inputs to that sector. Balanced technological change would occur if, for example, technological change increased the productivity of labor and other exogenous or primary factors uniformly in each sector (for copper mining, haircuts, jazz concerts, computers, and so forth), and if the earnings of labor and other primary factors increased by exactly that uniform rate of technological advance. In technical language, if all technological change were purely primary-factor augmenting at a uniform rate in each sector, and if real wages and the returns on all exogenous inputs rose at that rate (as they would under perfect competition), then the prices and allocations calculated in the base case would continue to hold.[7]

From historical examples we know that technological change has not generally been of the balanced variety. Many industries have shown persistently high rates of technological advance—particularly durable manufacturing, electricity generation, and communications. Other industries, such as services and construction, have shown relatively low rates of technological advance. Metal mining showed total factory productivity (TFP) growth of 0.6 percentage points per annum greater than the total economy over the period 1889 to 1953, although little of this productivity growth arose from dramatic breakthroughs in mining technology (see Kendrick 1961:136). And new products and processes have obviously shown extremely high rates of technological advance, for in these cases certain products previously unknown or not producible became commercially feasible. To the extent that different industries show different rates of productivity growth technological change is "unbalanced."

What would be a realistic assumption to make about technological change in the copper model? As we have emphasized elsewhere, it is impossible to foresee future inventions; for this reason, we chose not to speculate on future technological changes in our base case and instead assumed that they would be balanced. In our sensitivity runs, however, we were more venturesome. First, we know that by definition successful new processes and products will show relatively more rapid technological advance than existing products and processes. We would therefore expect that at least some new materials and processes will arise to replace those that we have enumerated. We will further guess that many of the new processes and products are likely to embody superabundant materials.

As an example, consider technological change in the transmission of telecommunications services. The effect of many of the important technological advances of the last half-century has been to replace existing copper-based technologies. Four such advances were microwave relay, multiplexing of signals, use of communications satellites, and fiber optics. In each case a new technology with significantly lower use of copper per unit output showed a much higher rate of technological advance than did the existing copper-based technology. To investigate the potential impact of differential technological advance on the supply of copper-equivalent services, we calculated the impact of different rates of *unbalanced* technological advance on our copper model. Although there are a wide variety of different cases, we take a very simple example.

Sensitivity run on technological change. We assume that all costs—of extraction, substitution, and recycling of copper, as well as those of alternative materials—change at the same rate each year. The base case sets that rate at zero. In the sensitivity runs that follow, the postulated rates of unbalanced technological change in copper and related industries are variously assumed to be -1, $+1$, $+2$, and $+4$ percent per annum. These figures were taken as representative of the differential rates of technological change in different industries (see, for example, Kendrick 1961). Over the last 100 years, most extractive industries have shown rates of measured productivity growth around 1 percent per annum greater than the economy as a whole. A few (such as electrical utilities, communications, and computers in their early stages) have shown rates of productivity growth as high as 8 percent per annum for a decade or two. Some unfortunate industries, such as nuclear power or coal mining in the early 1970s, have actually shown technological regression.

Our hunch, based on knowledge of materials and their uses and on past experience, is that in the future the production of copper services will show differential technological advance in the 1–2 percent range. Such high rates of productivity growth are likely to be attributable to the utilization of copper and substitute materials and from invention and diffusion of new products and processes rather than to improvements in the technology of extraction. We would be very surprised if the rate of technological advance were greater than 4 percent per annum or less than -1 percent per annum. The figures in Table 5.10 are upper and lower bounds on the impacts of technological change on our base case.

In addition, purely for computational simplicity, we have changed the discount rate by an equal amount in the opposite direction from the rate of technological advance. As can be seen from Table 5.8 and 5.9, this change has very little effect upon the path of prices and quantities.

The results shown in Table 5.10 indicate that technological advance may have a significant effect on the prices of copper metal and copper-equivalent services. If technological advance is around 2 percent per annum, the price of copper metal will grow very little over the next century. Moreover, in this case, the price of copper services will actually decline by a factor of two. In other words, given a rate of technological change of 2 percent per annum, the effects of technological advance and substitution will more than offset the effect of resource exhaustion in our base case.

Table 5.10   Impact of technological advance on the prices of copper metal and services

Variable	Period (decade)		Assumed rate of technological advance (% per annum)				
			-1	0	$+1$	$+2$	$+4$
Copper metal[a]							
	1	1970–1979	2.44	2.44	2.44	2.44	2.44
	6	2020–2029	22.5	13.69	8.28	4.98	1.78
	11	2070–2079	304.0	113.0	41.2	14.9	1.90
	14	2100–2109	442.0	121.0	33.3	9.13	0.74
Copper services[b]							
	1	1970–1979	100.0	100.0	100.0	100.0	100.0
	2	2020–2029	257.0	156.0	95.1	58.1	22.0
	3	2070–2079	1,690.0	623.0	230.0	86.1	12.3
	4	2100–2109	2,590.0	711.0	195.0	54.2	4.3

a. $ per kg.

b. $ per kg copper-equivalent; value-weighted arithmetic index, I_2 (1970–1979 = 100).

If the rate of technological change is extremely high, 4 percent per annum, then the price of copper metal will actually decline over the coming years, while the price of copper-equivalent services will fall very sharply. If we are unfortunate enough to experience technological regression in the copper sector, the dismal outlook of the base case becomes even gloomier.

It is useful to compare the uncertainty induced by technological change with the uncertainties due to other variables (compare Table 5.9 with Table 5.10). If we examine the impact on price in 2070–2079, we see that the range of uncertainty induced by technological change is between $2 and $305 per kilogram. This compares with a range of $22 to $240 per kilogram induced by other individual variables shown in Table 5.9. Clearly, then, the uncertainty about future technical advances is the most important single uncertainty that we have identified.

Copper Scarcity in a Macroeconomic Perspective

We now turn to a macroeconomic question: How important is the intrinsic scarcity of copper relative to the entire economy? Put another way, how much of a drag on economic growth will be caused by the limitation of high-grade copper resources?

We have already pointed out the consequences of copper's scarcity—the move to high-cost ores, the introduction of more costly substitutes, and expensive recycling. To estimate the overall impact of copper scarcity on the economy, we perform two hypothetical experiments. First, we ask what would occur if the scarcity of copper were suddenly to disappear—if, say, a giant deposit of 10^{15} kilogram of copper metal were suddenly found, or if a process for synthesizing copper metal from sand at $2 per kilogram were invented. The other experiment is to ask how much the ability to use copper is worth to a modern industrial economy. Imagine that a massive cloud of copper antimatter were to sweep across the planet and estimate the impact on economic activity of copper's subsequent disappearance.

An intuitive appraisal of the two scenarios appears in Figure 5.11 and the accompanying legend; a more rigorous definition of the concepts behind it is as follows. Let $Y(c_t, A_t)$ be the flow of gross output as a function of the services of copper, c_t, and substitutes, A_t. The costs of extracting and delivering copper and substitutes are represented by a cost function, $F(c_t, A_t)$. Thus, net output, X_t, is given by

$$(5.1) \qquad X(c_t, A_t) = Y(c_t, A_t) - F(c_t, A_t).$$

Using continuous time for notational simplicity, we set up the LP program to maximize an objective function of total discounted net output, V:

$$(5.2) \qquad V = \int_0^T X(c_t, A_t) R(t) dt,$$

where $R(t)$ is the appropriate discount factor. In addition, there is an auxiliary constraint on the availability of copper. We maximize V under the two assumptions about copper availability discussed above and the base case as represented by the model. In each case the value of the objective function corresponds to the maximum feasible level of V subject to the relevant constraint about copper supply.

To estimate the impact of "superabundant copper" and "copper disappearance," we performed the following calculations. We calculated V for our base case, then compared the result with V for case 9 above ("Remove copper scarcity," which corresponds to the trajectory "superabundant

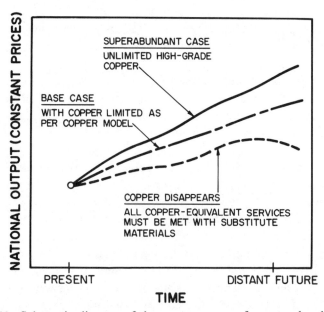

Figure 5.11 Schematic diagram of the consequences of copper abundance and scarcity in a macroeconomic context. The upper, solid curve shows the trajectory of national copper output assuming that copper is superabundant at current ore grades. The middle line shows the trajectory along the path of economic growth as estimated in the base case. The bottom line shows the effect of meeting the demand for all copper services with substitute materials. We estimate the drag on economic growth from copper exhaustion by examining the differences between the paths.

copper'') and for case 10 ("Copper disappears," which corresponds to the lowest trajectory in Figure 5.11). For each case we calculated the discounted future cost of providing all copper-equivalent services over the next 180 years. We then compared the cost of providing the same services in each of the three runs.

The results of modifying the base-case assumptions on copper availability are shown in Table 5.11. In the base case, the intrinsic scarcity of copper implies that meeting the demand for copper-equivalent services over the next 180 years will require $151 billion more in additional costs of capital and labor than would be required if copper were superabundant at current costs. In other words, we calculate that meeting the demand for copper will cost approximately $151 billion more in resources—as the United States moves to higher-cost substitutes, to greater recycling, and to the mining of low-grade ores—under present conditions than if we were able to find an infinite vein of high-grade ores. Over the 180-year period of the copper model, this increase amounts to 0.4 percent of the discounted value of national income as measured by Net National Product (NNP).

Is this number—$151 billion or 0.4 percent of the discounted value of NNP over the next 180 years—large or small? It strikes us as somewhere in between. It is of the same order of magnitude as the economic cost of protectionism, the losses from monopoly, or the cost of regulation.[8] It is certainly not a trivial figure; as the famous senator might have said, a few percent of GNP here, a few percent there, and it begins to add up to real losses. On the other hand, the cost of copper scarcity falls short of the apocalyptic visions seen by *The Limits to Growth* and the Doomsday models.

The estimate for the event that copper disappears is at first blush astounding. Our calculation suggests that if we were to provide the projected

Table 5.11   Impact of copper scarcity on costs

Case	Discounted costs over 180-year period (billions of dollars, 1978 prices)	Difference from base case	
		Billions of dollars, 1978 prices	Percentage of discounted NNP
Base case	419	0	0
Superabundant case	267	151	0.4
Copper disappears	8,859	−8,440	−22.1

Table 5.12 Effect of copper scarcity on real income, 1970–2150[a]

Run	Case	Description	Change from super-abundant case[a] (billions of dollars, 1978 prices) (1)	(1) as percentage of NNP[b] (2)
0	00	Base case	151	0.4%
		Alternative economic growth		
03	2A	Slow economic growth	—	—
04	2B	Rapid economic growth	—	—
		Discount rate		
08	6A	Increase by 2%	—	—
09	6B	Decrease by 2%	—	—
		Geology		
05	3A	No backstop ores	197	0.5
06	3B	Backstop cost × 4	183	0.5
07	3C	Backstop cost × 0.25	111	0.3
13	3D	Double extraction costs	280	0.7
18	3E	Resources × 0.5	277	0.7
17	3F	Resources × 1.5	106	0.3

11	4C	Eliminate recycling	396	1.0
		Substitution		
19	5A	Double substitution costs	352	0.9
20	5B	Halve substitution costs	-222	-0.7
15	5C	Decrease electronic wire substitution costs	-98	-0.3
16	5D	Increase miscellaneous substitution costs	606	1.6
24	7A	Pessimistic case	851	2.2
25	7B	Very pessimistic case	—	—
26	8A	Optimistic case	—	—
27	8B	Very optimistic case	—	—

a. The figure in column (1) is derived from the value of the objective function. More precisely, let V_i = the attained minimum value of the objective function for run i; let V_s = the attained minimum value for the superabundant case. Column (1) equals $V_i - V_s$. That is, it is equal to the extra discounted present and future cost that must be paid to meet the copper-equivalent services when the model is run according to the assumptions of case i as compared with the superabundant case. For example, the total cost of meeting present and future demand is \$151 billion more in the base case than in the superabundant case.

b. For these calculations, real income is taken as the discounted present value for U.S. NNP, using the discounting and growth assumptions in the model.

copper-equivalent services over the next 180 years entirely with substitutes for copper, the additional cost would amount to 22 percent of NNP. In technical economic language, the discounted consumer and producer surplus that arises from copper's availability is 22 percent of discounted NNP.[9] This figure might at first appear surprisingly large. Yet when we recall the ubiquity of copper—in cars and motors, in telephone lines and electrical wiring, in power generation and electronic calculators—and when we contemplate the difficulty of operating some of these with alternatives, then the immensity of nature's bounty arising from the availability of copper may seem quite plausible.

Finally, we have performed for the various cases we proposed sensitivity analyses of the effect on V of a superabundance of copper (see Table 5.12). Column (1) demonstrates how much more it costs to provide the copper-equivalent services in the particular run examined than providing those services costs in run 21. We call this "the cost of copper scarcity." In the second column, we calculate the cost of copper scarcity as a percent of total discounted future NNP over the same period for each sensitivity run.[10] Most of the estimates lie in the range 0.1 to 0.7 percent of NNP. Only in outlying cases do we find that the cost of copper scarcity substantially exceeds 1 percent of NNP.

Appendix

Table 5A.1   Computed pattern of efficient extraction of copper ores

Period	Decade	Annual extraction[a] (millions of tons per year)	Cumulative[a] (millions of tons)	Resource categories used[b]
1	1970–1979	1.74	17.4	1– 3
2	1980–1989	2.78	45.2	1– 5
3	1990–1999	3.74	82.6	4– 7
4	2000–2009	4.93	132.0	5–10
5	2010–2019	6.58	198.0	7–12
6	2020–2029	9.13	289.0	10–14
7	2030–2039	5.96	349.0	12–16
8	2040–2049	6.89	418.0	15–21
9	2050–2059	8.70	505.0	16–21
		Backstop resource reached		
10	2060–2069	11.41	619.0	21–22
11	2070–2079	8.42	703.0	22–22
12	2080–2089	9.82	801.0	22–22
13	2090–2099	15.8	960.0	22–22
14	2100–2109	11.3	1,070.0	22–22
15	2110–2119	14.6	1,220.0	22–22
16	2120–2129	9.36	1,310.0	22–22
17	2130–2139	10.6	1,420.0	22–22
18	2140–2149	10.6	1,520.0	22–22

a. A ton represents 1,000 kg or 1.1 short tons.
b. Resource categories are defined in Table 2.5.

Table 5A.2   Substitution patterns by demand category: share of the substitute as

Demand category	Substitute material	1970–1979	1980–1989	1990–1999	2000–2009	2010–2019	2020–2029	2030–2039
1. Radiators	Aluminum	7.9	49.4	80.3	100.0	100.0	100.0	100.0
2. Refrigeration	Aluminum	43.5	75.9	100.0	100.0	100.0	100.0	100.0
3. Industrial heat exchangers	Titanium	0.0	0.0	0.0	0.0	0.0	0.0	0.0
4. Power transmission cable	Aluminum	43.5	75.9	100.0	100.0	100.0	100.0	100.0
5. Building wire	Aluminum	43.5	75.9	100.0	100.0	100.0	100.0	100.0
6. Electronic wire	Aluminum	0.0	0.0	0.0	0.0	0.0	0.0	0.0
7. Motors, < 1 HP	Aluminum	0.0	0.0	0.0	0.0	0.0	0.0	0.0
8. Motors, 1–20 HP	Aluminum	0.0	0.0	0.0	0.0	0.0	0.0	0.0
9. Motors, > 20 HP	Aluminum	0.0	0.0	0.0	0.0	0.0	0.0	0.0
10. Transformers	Aluminum	43.5	75.9	100.0	100.0	100.0	100.0	100.0
11. Pipe	Plastic	43.5	75.9	100.0	100.0	100.0	100.0	100.0
12. Castings	Stainless steel	0.0	0.0	0.0	0.0	0.0	0.0	43.5
13. Forgings	Stainless steel	43.5	75.9	100.0	100.0	100.0	100.0	100.0
14. Machinery	Stainless steel	0.0	0.0	0.0	0.0	0.0	17.1	56.3
15. Ordnance	Carbon steel	0.0	43.5	75.9	100.0	100.0	100.0	100.0
16. Coinage	Zinc	43.5	75.9	100.0	100.0	100.0	100.0	100.0
17. Communication T4	Optic fiber	0.0	0.0	0.0	0.0	0.0	0.0	0.0
18. Communication T3	Optic fiber	0.0	0.0	0.0	0.0	0.0	0.0	0.0
19. Communication T2	Optic fiber	0.0	0.0	0.0	0.0	0.0	0.0	0.0
20. Communication T1	Optic fiber	0.0	0.0	0.0	0.0	0.0	0.0	0.0
21. Communication LL	Optic fiber	0.0	0.0	0.0	0.0	0.0	0.0	0.0

percentage of total demand

2040–2049	2050–2059	2060–2069	2070–2079	2080–2089	2090–2099	2100–2109	2110–2119	2120–2129	2130–2139	2140–2149
100.0	100.0	100.0	100.0	100.0	100.0	100.0	100.0	100.0	100.0	100.0
100.0	100.0	100.0	100.0	100.0	100.0	100.0	100.0	100.0	100.0	100.0
0.0	0.0	43.5	39.4	35.7	9.4	23.2	21.0	52.5	70.3	100.0
100.0	100.0	100.0	100.0	100.0	100.0	100.0	100.0	100.0	100.0	100.0
100.0	100.0	100.0	100.0	100.0	100.0	100.0	100.0	100.0	100.0	100.0
0.0	0.0	0.0	0.0	0.0	0.0	0.0	0.0	0.0	0.0	0.0
43.5	75.9	100.0	100.0	100.0	100.0	100.0	100.0	100.0	100.0	100.0
0.0	0.0	43.5	70.7	100.0	100.0	100.0	100.0	100.0	100.0	100.0
0.0	0.0	39.9	36.1	32.7	0.0	0.0	0.0	40.5	70.3	100.0
100.0	100.0	100.0	100.0	100.0	100.0	100.0	100.0	100.0	100.0	100.0
100.0	100.0	100.0	100.0	100.0	100.0	100.0	100.0	100.0	100.0	100.0
75.9	100.0	100.0	100.0	100.0	100.0	100.0	100.0	100.0	100.0	100.0
100.0	100.0	100.0	100.0	100.0	100.0	100.0	100.0	100.0	100.0	100.0
85.4	100.0	100.0	100.0	100.0	100.0	100.0	100.0	100.0	100.0	100.0
100.0	100.0	100.0	100.0	100.0	100.0	100.0	100.0	100.0	100.0	100.0
100.0	100.0	100.0	100.0	100.0	100.0	100.0	100.0	100.0	100.0	100.0
0.0	0.0	0.0	0.0	0.0	0.0	0.0	0.0	0.0	0.0	0.0
0.0	0.0	0.0	0.0	0.0	0.0	0.0	0.0	0.0	0.0	0.0
0.0	0.0	43.6	70.7	100.0	100.0	100.0	100.0	100.0	100.0	100.0
43.5	75.9	100.0	100.0	100.0	100.0	100.0	100.0	100.0	100.0	100.0
43.5	75.9	100.0	100.0	100.0	100.0	100.0	100.0	100.0	100.0	100.0

Table 5A.3 Recycling patterns for each scrap category

Period	Decade	Building	Transport	Contribution of scrap to copper deliveries[a]			
				Consumer goods	Industrial Equipment	Electric & electronic	Coinage
1	1970–1979	21.06	3.70	1.89	9.88	13.36	0.54
2	1980–1989	12.52	2.20	1.12	5.87	7.94	0.32
3	1990–1999	12.52	2.20	1.12	5.87	7.94	0.32
4	2000–2009	1.93	8.56	5.21	9.97	4.91	0.68
5	2010–2019	1.93	4.08	3.82	9.97	11.95	0.0
6	2020–2029	1.99	4.22	3.95	10.30	6.77	0.0
7	2030–2039	2.71	5.73	5.36	29.02	9.19	0.0
8	2040–2049	5.00	13.93	5.84	20.30	10.00	0.0
9	2050–2059	7.37	7.99	12.27	19.98	9.68	0.47
10	2060–2069	0.0	9.73	9.05	15.84	11.93	0.0
11	2070–2079	0.0	13.49	12.50	21.96	11.34	0.0
12	2080–2089	0.0	14.26	13.21	23.21	11.99	0.0
13	2090–2099	0.0	12.93	12.84	13.22	12.85	0.0
14	2100–2109	0.0	13.13	12.07	22.20	12.08	0.0
15	2110–2119	0.0	13.04	11.99	22.05	11.99	0.0
16	2120–2129	0.0	16.66	15.32	26.49	15.32	0.0
17	2130–2139	0.0	15.64	14.38	23.28	14.39	0.0
18	2140–2149	0.0	16.08	14.78	27.19	14.79	0.0

a. Entry is recycling from each scrap category as percentage of total deliveries of copper metal.

Table 5A.4   Recycling and stocks of copper (millions of tons, copper metal)

Period	Decade	Amount of copper recycled	Amount of copper unrecycled	Stock of scrap available
1	1970–1979	17.72	6.85	24.5
2	1980–1989	11.91	11.46	23.3
3	1990–1999	16.01	17.65	33.6
4	2000–2009	22.43	23.34	45.7
5	2010–2019	30.62	24.50	55.1
6	2020–2029	34.16	33.05	67.2
7	2030–2039	64.57	25.88	90.4
8	2040–2049	84.42	18.61	103.0
9	2050–2059	119.01	0.0	119.0
10	2060–2069	99.34	0.0	99.3
11	2070–2079	122.65	0.0	122.6
12	2080–2089	164.83	0.0	164.8
13	2090–2099	170.73	0.0	170.7
14	2100–2109	165.47	0.0	165.4
15	2110–2119	210.40	0.0	210.4
16	2120–2129	263.51	0.0	263.5
17	2130–2139	222.56	0.0	222.5
18	2140–2149	284.98	0.0	284.9

Table 5A.5 Aggregate material flow and stock balance (millions of tons, copper or copper-equivalent)

Period	Decade	Deliveries (per year)			Stock	
		Mining	Recycling	Substitute	Copper	Substitute
1	1970–1979	17.4	17.7	127.0	245.5	127.0
2	1980–1989	27.8	11.9	178.1	195.5	305.1
3	1990–1999	37.4	16.0	239.4	128.3	544.5
4	2000–2009	49.3	22.4	321.7	164.9	739.2
5	2010–2019	65.8	30.6	432.3	221.6	993.4
6	2020–2029	91.3	34.2	585.1	293.7	1339.2
7	2030–2039	59.6	64.6	830.8	346.1	1848.3
8	2040–2049	68.9	84.4	1130.1	403.0	2546.1
9	2050–2059	87.0	119.0	1518.8	483.5	3479.8
10	2060–2069	114.1	99.3	2104.6	572.8	4753.6
11	2070–2079	84.2	122.7	1633.8	626.3	5257.3
12	2080–2089	98.2	164.8	2077.4	683.3	5815.8
13	2090–2099	158.7	170.7	2668.6	799.2	6379.8
14	2100–2109	112.7	165.5	2313.5	870.6	7059.4
15	2110–2119	145.8	210.4	2813.7	963.8	7795.8
16	2120–2129	93.6	263.5	3557.2	991.5	8684.4
17	2130–2139	106.2	222.6	3275.1	1042.1	9646.1
18	2140–2149	106.2	285.0	3896.9	1077.1	10729.2

Table 5A.6   Aggregate material flow and stock balance as percentage of share

Period	Decade	Deliveries (per year)			Stock	
		Mining	Recycling	Substitute	Copper	Substitute
1	1970–1979	10.8	10.9	78.3	65.9	34.1
2	1980–1989	12.8	5.5	81.8	39.1	60.9
3	1990–1999	12.8	5.5	81.8	19.1	80.9
4	2000–2009	12.5	5.7	81.8	18.2	81.8
5	2010–2019	12.4	5.8	81.8	18.2	81.8
6	2020–2029	12.9	4.8	82.3	18.0	82.0
7	2030–2039	6.2	6.8	87.0	15.8	84.2
8	2040–2049	5.4	6.6	88.1	13.7	86.3
9	2050–2059	5.0	6.9	88.1	12.2	87.8
10	2060–2069	4.9	4.3	90.8	10.8	89.2
11	2070–2079	4.6	6.7	88.8	10.6	89.4
12	2080–2089	4.2	7.0	88.8	10.5	89.5
13	2090–2099	5.3	5.7	89.0	11.1	88.9
14	2100–2109	4.3	6.4	89.3	11.0	89.0
15	2110–2119	4.6	6.6	88.8	11.0	89.0
16	2120–2129	2.4	6.7	90.9	10.2	89.8
17	2130–2139	2.9	6.2	90.9	9.8	90.2
18	2140–2149	2.5	6.6	90.9	9.1	90.9

Table 5A.7 Scarcity rents on copper resource in the ground (U.S. dollars per kg, 1978 prices)

Grade of the copper resource	1970–1979	1980–1989	1990–1999	2000–2009	2010–2019	2020–2029	2030–2039	2040–2049	2050–2059	2060–2069
1	0.930	2.008	e[a]	e	e	e	e	e	e	e
2	0.744	1.607	e	e	e	e	e	e	e	e
3	0.559	1.206	e	e	e	e	e	e	e	e
4	0.459	0.992	2.141	e	e	e	e	e	e	e
5	0.373	0.806	1.740	3.75	e	e	e	e	e	e
6	0.313	0.677	1.461	3.15	e	e	e	e	e	e
7	0.273	0.590	1.275	2.75	5.94	e	e	e	e	e
8	0.255	0.551	1.189	2.56	5.54	e	e	e	e	e
9	0.237	0.511	1.103	2.38	5.14	e	e	e	e	e
10	0.218	0.471	1.016	2.19	4.73	10.22	e	e	e	e
11	0.205	0.443	0.956	2.06	4.45	9.62	e	e	e	e
12	0.188	0.406	0.877	1.89	4.08	8.82	19.0	e	e	e

13	0.180	0.389	0.840	1.81	3.91	8.44	18.2	e	e	e
14	0.172	0.372	0.803	1.73	3.74	8.07	17.4	e	e	e
15	0.168	0.362	0.782	1.68	3.64	7.87	16.9	36.6	e	e
16	0.162	0.350	0.757	1.63	3.52	7.61	16.4	35.4	76.6	e
17	0.159	0.343	0.741	1.59	3.45	7.45	16.0	34.7	74.9	e
18	0.156	0.336	0.725	1.56	3.37	7.29	15.7	33.9	73.3	e
19	0.150	0.325	0.701	1.51	3.26	7.05	15.2	32.8	70.9	e
20	0.135	0.291	0.628	1.35	2.92	6.31	13.6	29.4	63.5	e
21	0.122	0.263	0.568	1.22	2.64	5.71	12.3	26.6	57.5	124.202
22[b]	0.0	0.0	0.0	0.0	0.0	0.0	0.0	0.0	0.0	0.0
A[c]	0.559	0.806	1.275	2.194	4.086	8.077	16.435	26.647	57.530	0.0
B[c]	2.439	3.169	4.267	5.932	8.715	13.686	23.399	42.534	83.464	128.445
C[c]	0.229	0.254	0.299	0.370	0.469	0.590	0.702	0.626	0.689	0.0

a. Resource of the grade is exhausted.

b. Grade 22 is the backstop grade.

c. A, Scarcity rent on marginal grade; B, price of copper; C, ratio of scarcity rent on marginal grade to price.

Table 5A.8 Prices of copper or copper-equivalent services in each demand sector

Demand category	Substitute material	Prices of copper or copper-equivalent service ($/kg)[a]						
		1970– 1979	1980– 1989	1990– 1999	2000– 2009	2010– 2019	2020– 2029	2030– 2039
1. Radiators	Aluminum	1.25	1.25	1.25	1.25	1.25	1.26	1.22
2. Refrigeration	Aluminum	0.44	0.44	0.44	0.43	0.44	0.44	0.43
3. Industrial heat exchangers	Titanium	1.09	1.34	1.76	2.12	2.67	3.97	4.49
4. Power transmission cable	Aluminum	(a)[b]	(a)	(a)	(a)	(a)	(a)	(a)
5. Building wire	Aluminum	(a)	(a)	(a)	(a)	(a)	(a)	(a)
6. Electronic wire	Aluminum	1.10	1.34	1.74	2.20	2.68	3.72	5.16
7. Motors, < 1 HP	Aluminum	1.12	1.44	1.64	2.18	3.44	2.47	4.71
8. Motors, 1–20 HP	Aluminum	1.09	1.35	1.86	1.99	2.69	4.83	2.89
9. Motors, > 20 HP	Aluminum	1.10	1.34	1.74	2.18	2.68	3.72	5.04
10. Transformers	Aluminum	0.89	0.89	0.89	0.89	0.89	0.90	0.87
11. Pipe	Plastic	0.93	0.93	0.93	0.93	0.93	0.94	0.91
12. Castings	Stainless steel	1.11	1.36	1.63	2.36	2.85	2.56	6.79
13. Forgings	Stainless steel	0.64	0.64	0.64	0.64	0.64	0.65	0.63
14. Machinery	Stainless steel	1.10	1.34	1.81	2.11	2.59	4.36	4.22
15. Ordnance	Carbon steel	1.14	1.49	1.50	1.49	1.50	1.51	1.46
16. Coinage	Zinc	0.89	0.89	0.89	0.88	0.89	0.89	0.86
17. Communication T4	Optic fiber	1.09	1.32	1.71	2.16	2.64	3.66	5.11
18. Communication T3	Optic fiber	1.09	1.32	1.71	2.16	2.64	3.66	5.11
19. Communication T2	Optic fiber	1.06	1.31	1.83	1.91	2.60	4.91	2.60
20. Communication T1	Optic fiber	1.07	1.40	1.59	2.04	3.46	2.44	3.90
21. Communication LL	Optic fiber	1.08	1.39	1.57	2.14	3.32	2.28	4.92

a. All prices are constant-dollar prices, i.e., deflated by estimated value of GNP deflator relative to 1978.

b. (a), in categories 4 and 5, copper use is less efficient than the substitute in first period, so price is not meaningful.

Prices of copper or copper-equivalent service ($/kg)[a]										
2040–2049	2050–2059	2060–2069	2070–2079	2080–2089	2090–2099	2100–2109	2110–2119	2120–2129	2130–2139	2140–2149
1.27	1.36	0.96	0.96	1.09	0.89	0.89	1.33	0.68	0.68	2.10
0.44	0.47	0.33	0.33	0.38	0.31	0.31	0.46	0.24	0.24	0.73
5.32	29.72	49.33	33.89	46.28	39.62	41.14	56.81	30.28	30.28	93.34
(a)	(a)	(a)	(a)	(a)	(a)	(a)	(a)	(a)	(a)	(a)
(a)	(a)	(a)	(a)	(a)	(a)	(a)	(a)	(a)	(a)	(a)
5.30	26.91	55.87	33.58	44.42	43.45	39.94	50.60	42.51	26.18	132.04
12.69	13.61	9.58	9.58	10.94	8.93	8.93	13.32	6.83	6.83	21.05
5.22	37.84	32.91	32.91	37.55	30.68	30.68	45.74	23.45	23.45	72.28
5.35	27.15	54.81	34.07	45.69	40.16	41.69	54.88	32.01	32.01	98.68
0.90	0.97	0.68	0.68	0.78	0.64	0.64	0.95	0.49	0.49	1.50
0.94	1.01	0.71	0.71	0.81	0.66	0.66	0.99	0.51	0.51	1.56
7.03	7.54	5.31	5.31	6.06	4.95	4.95	7.38	3.78	3.78	11.66
0.65	0.70	0.49	0.49	0.56	0.46	0.46	0.68	0.35	0.35	1.08
4.37	4.69	3.30	3.30	3.77	3.08	3.08	4.59	2.35	2.35	7.25
1.51	1.62	1.14	1.14	1.30	1.06	1.06	1.59	0.81	0.81	2.51
0.90	0.96	0.68	0.68	0.77	0.63	0.63	0.94	0.48	0.48	1.49
5.23	26.80	55.73	33.44	44.21	43.34	39.83	50.27	42.51	26.18	132.04
5.23	26.80	55.73	33.44	44.21	43.34	39.83	50.27	42.51	26.18	132.04
4.81	39.40	30.51	30.51	34.81	28.44	28.44	42.39	21.74	21.74	67.00
13.53	14.52	10.22	10.22	11.66	9.53	9.53	14.20	7.28	7.28	22.45
12.06	12.93	9.11	9.11	10.39	8.49	8.49	12.65	6.49	6.49	20.00

Table 5A.9   Shadow price of scrap heaps (dollars per kg copper metal)

Kind of scrap heap	No.	1970–1979	1980–1989	1990–1999	2000–2009	2010–2019	2020–2029	2030–2039	2040–2049
Buildings	1	2.291	3.022	4.11	5.78	8.56	13.5	23.2	42.3
	2	1.820	2.551	3.64	5.31	8.09	13.0	22.7	41.9
	3	0.720	1.451	2.54	4.21	6.99	11.9	21.6	40.8
	4	0.162	0.349	0.75	1.62	2.51	7.5	16.3	35.3
Transport	5	2.292	3.023	4.12	5.78	8.56	13.5	23.2	42.3
	6	1.823	2.554	3.65	5.31	8.09	13.0	22.7	41.9
	7	0.729	1.459	2.55	4.22	7.00	11.9	21.6	40.8
	8	0.162	0.349	0.75	1.62	3.51	7.5	16.3	35.3
Consumer	9	2.152	2.882	3.98	5.64	8.42	13.3	23.1	42.2
	10	1.233	1.964	3.06	4.72	7.51	12.4	22.1	41.3
	11	0.257	0.554	1.19	2.58	5.36	10.3	20.0	39.1
	12	0.147	0.317	0.68	1.48	3.19	6.8	14.8	32.1
Industrial equipment	13	2.329	3.060	4.15	5.82	8.60	13.5	23.2	42.4
	14	1.977	2.708	3.80	5.47	8.25	13.2	22.9	42.0
	15	1.157	1.888	2.98	4.65	7.43	12.4	22.1	41.2
	16	0.178	0.384	0.82	1.79	3.86	8.3	18.0	37.1
Electric and electronic	17	2.366	3.097	4.19	5.85	8.64	13.6	23.2	42.4
	18	2.133	2.864	3.96	5.62	8.41	13.3	23.0	42.2
	19	1.590	2.321	3.41	5.08	7.86	12.8	22.5	41.6
	20	0.237	0.512	1.10	2.38	5.15	10.1	19.8	38.9
Coinage	21	1.724	2.455	3.55	5.21	8.00	12.9	22.6	41.8
	22	0.291	0.629	1.35	2.93	5.71	10.6	23.0	49.8
	23	0.159	0.344	0.74	1.60	3.45	7.4	16.1	34.8
	24	0.103	0.222	0.47	1.03	2.23	4.8	10.3	22.4

2050–2059	2060–2069	2070–2079	2080–2089	2090–2099	2100–2109	2110–2119	2120–2129	2130–2139	2140–2149
83.3	179	112	121	180	121	123	120	115	131
82.8	127	112	121	121	120	122	119	114	131
81.7	126	187	120	120	119	121	118	113	130
76.2	164	105	114	115	114	115	113	167	124
83.3	128	112	121	122	121	123	120	115	131
82.8	127	112	121	121	120	122	119	114	131
81.7	126	111	120	120	119	121	118	113	130
76.2	121	105	114	115	114	116	113	108	124
83.1	128	112	121	122	121	122	120	115	131
82.2	127	111	120	121	120	122	119	114	130
80.1	125	109	118	119	118	119	117	112	128
69.4	114	98	107	108	107	109	106	101	117
83.3	128	112	121	122	121	123	120	115	131
83.0	127	112	121	122	120	122	120	114	131
82.1	127	111	120	121	120	121	119	114	130
78.0	123	107	116	117	115	117	115	110	126
83.3	128	112	121	122	121	123	120	115	131
83.1	128	112	121	122	121	122	120	115	131
82.6	127	111	120	121	120	122	119	114	131
79.9	124	109	118	119	117	119	116	111	128
82.7	127	112	121	121	120	122	119	114	131
80.4	125	109	118	119	118	120	117	112	129
75.1	120	104	113	114	113	114	112	107	123
48.4	93	138	204	303	448	88	85	80	97

6 Toward a New Iron Age

Our sortie into copper's past, present, and possible future has covered much ground. In this final chapter we will briefly survey the terrain, explaining what we encountered and why. We begin with a review of the copper model and an analysis of some of the pitfalls of projecting future patterns of exhaustion. In the second half of the chapter we extrapolate the results to consider the consequences of the exhaustion of scarce mineral resources other than copper. Finally, we speculate on how mineral exhaustion may hinder future economic development.

The Findings for Copper

The Materials-Modeling Approach

In this study we have proposed and implemented a new approach to analyzing the economics of the use of materials obtained from limited resources, an approach we call materials modeling. In the language of econometrics, this method is highly structural, relying to the greatest possible extent on technological and scientific data rather than on projections of past events into the future.

Our purpose in making the study was to investigate the intrinsic scarcity of copper—that is, the scarcity of copper as an economic commodity and the ways in which an efficient pattern of exhaustion of copper resources would unfold over time.[1] To calculate scarcity and exhaustion patterns, we built a mathematical optimization model of the availability and use of copper. This model uses a linear-programming framework to minimize the total cost of meeting a predetermined path of services provided by copper or its substitutes (here called copper-equivalent services). We have shown that this approach is justified by the correspondence principle that applies between competitive markets and optimization.

The ingredients in the model are (1) the geologic availability of copper ores in deposits of different grades, depths, and sizes; (2) the cost of using copper or substitute materials in serving a wide variety of purposes, such as piping water, conducting electricity, and transmitting information; (3) the cost of recycling discarded copper; (4) the technology by which the capital stock of copper or substitute materials is used to provide demanded services; and (5) the exogenously given time paths of the demand for services.

The results of the maximization were set out fully in Chapter 5. We will recapitulate them in brief terms first, beginning with the results obtained for the base case, which was run over the time period 1970 to 2150.

1. The rate of extraction of copper from the earth grows rapidly over the next 100 years. Extraction peaks in about the year 2100 and then declines slowly. The peak extraction rate is about eight times the current rate of production of new copper.

2. The ores containing copper minerals are largely exhausted by about 2070. Thereafter, copper is obtained from common rock, which has a maximum grade of 0.05 percent, compared with the 0.5 percent of metal in the ore being mined today. When copper is obtained from common rock, the intrinsic scarcity of copper disappears; copper is then very expensive but no longer "scarce" in the sense of being exhaustible.

3. As time passes, the services currently or historically provided by copper are progressively provided by greater amounts of substitute materials such as aluminum, titanium, stainless steel, plastics, and glass. By the end of the twenty-first century, only a handful of today's uses of copper survive. Copper is so superior to possible substitutes that it continues to be used for electronic wiring, some electric motors, and some communications equipment, but by the end of the model period substitute materials provide 90 percent of the services now provided by copper.

4. Recycling becomes big business. In the next few decades, many scrapped products containing copper are not recycled, but by the middle of the next century virtually all copper available from junk is recovered and reused.

5. Copper prices rise dramatically over the next century. They follow the classic trajectory for an exhaustible resource, growing exponentially from about $2 per kilogram in early periods to $120 per kilogram when the backstop resources (common rock) are brought into play; thereafter, there is no further increase.

6. Even though the price of copper metal rises fiftyfold over the next century, the cost of copper-equivalent services rises only tenfold.

After modeling the base case we performed sensitivity analyses to determine how the outcome of the base case changes when key assumptions in the model are changed. Changes in some of the assumptions, such as in the time horizon used, have little effect on the results. The parameters to which the results are most sensitive are the projected economic growth over the next two centuries, the feasibility of using common rock as a superabundant copper resource, and the cost of substitution for copper in electronic wiring. The most important uncertainty, however, concerns technological advance. Our base case assumes balanced technological change for all sectors, processes, and products. If, as seems more likely, technological change in the use of copper substitutes proceeds relatively rapidly, then the prices for copper and copper services will rise more modestly than for the base case and may even decline.

Finally, we investigated the macroeconomic consequences of limited copper resources. The overall economic cost of copper scarcity, defined as the difference in the cost between the base case and a hypothetical case where copper is superabundant at today's prices, was estimated to be somewhat less than 0.5 percent of the total national income (both appropriately discounted). For this calculation we assumed that the superabundant (though costly) resources of copper and its substitutes can be used, that the energy and water required to process these resources are available, and that nearly all copper in use is recycled. The most remarkable result, however, was the estimated cost of the hypothetical complete disappearance of copper today. We found that the cost of doing without copper would be approximately 22 percent of the total national income. Thus, existing intrinsic scarcity of copper appears to be a relatively small cost, but to do completely without copper would place a heavy burden on our industrial economy.

Reservations

The assumptions required for the model inject an element of artificiality into the results, and we continue to harbor reservations about the methods employed and the projections made. The effects of some of our assumptions on the results have been tested with the sensitivity runs, but the consequences of other assumptions cannot be examined in this way.

The first reservation arises from our assumption that the future can be predicted with sufficient clarity to allow us to construct an economic model. The method presumes a rational, market-modulated reaction to each set of conditions imposed by geology, technology, or demand. Extreme events and irrational actions, such as a devastating war or the spread of a belief that the use of copper is evil, are ruled out. Despite these reservations, we believe that the major changes and steps predicted by the model represent the way copper resources are most likely to be used in the future. The magnitude and timing of major events may be inaccurate, but their quantitative characteristics seem to us to be the most likely description of future events.

A second limitation arises from assumptions in the model that may distort the results. The most obvious of these is treatment of the United States as an isolated entity, self-sufficient in copper throughout the time period of the model. Although the assumption of self-sufficiency is unrealistic, we think it affects our results only slightly. Exports and imports of copper will, of course, occur, but the needs for copper services will continue to rise in other countries as well, including those that are now net exporters of copper. The United States still has relatively rich copper resources. Other regions rich in copper are known, and more copper may be found in previously untested areas, such as Antarctica or the deep-sea floor. But all countries will have to draw from these resources in the future, and eventually all will have to draw on the backstop resources. Our assumption of an isolated, self-sufficient country is really an assumption that economic development in the United States is a microcosm for the industrial development of the world. We expect the sequence of events for the world as a whole will parallel our predictions for the United States, but the timing of events may be different.

A third and more important limitation of our approach arises from our inability to foresee future technological developments. The history of technology suggests that the most likely future development will be the invention of new materials or devices that make today's copper uses obsolete. Less likely in our view, but still possible, is the invention of new devices of such utility that they create vast new demands for copper. We simply cannot predict such events, yet we expect that some of them will happen.

But before we throw up our hands with a cry of complete ignorance, we ought to recall the shape of changes in copper-using technology over the past two centuries. During this period of enormous technological advance a vast array of new products and substitute materials appeared. Yet the overall use of copper has continued to increase even as aluminum, stainless steel, and plastics have eaten into copper's market, and we expect that this market erosion will continue. But the physical and chemical properties of copper make it ideal for many uses. Technological change will not alter this, and the use of substitutes will probably involve difficulties that do not plague copper. Experience suggests that these problems will be underestimated, as they were when aluminum was first used in place of copper for electrical wiring in houses.

The fourth set of reservations arises from our inability to predict political changes. Despite the development of major power blocs, trade between nations has continued to some extent at all times. Whether this will continue, or whether some country will choose to wield its control of inexpensive resources as either a strategic or a political tool, can be imagined but not predicted. We are confident that the end result of such a move would be to change only the timing of switch points, not our major conclusions.

The fifth and final set of reservations relates to two of our assumptions—first, that the substitute materials used to provide copper's services will be available without resource constraints, and second, that the consequences of the large-scale mining of common rock required to use the backstop resources for copper will be acceptable to society in the future. In a geo-chemical sense there is no doubt about the abundance of the substitute materials or of the copper backstop. But limitations on the use of these resources could arise from unwillingness to accept large-scale mining and its concomitant production of wastes and from scarcity of the water and energy required to process these low-grade resources.

We have made no attempt to assess the consequences of mining the superabundant resources of the substitute materials, but we anticipate that it will entail fewer problems than will mining backstop copper resources. Aluminum, titanium, and silicon, for example, are much more abundant in common rock than is copper. Energy requirements will become a more severe limitation as more substitutes are used, because the substitute materials require more energy to produce than copper—2.4 times as much for aluminum and 3.7 times as much for titanium per pound, for example. We cannot predict the reaction of society to the large-scale demands on energy and water resources that will be made by the use of either the substitute materials or the backstop resource of copper. We can imagine circumstances in which meeting such demands would be less preferable than putting up with the consequent reduced availability of materials for engineering and technology. Our sensitivity analyses provided a rough indication of the impact of such events.

Extrapolation of the Results

Is Copper a Unique Metal?

Copper could be viewed as a unique metal because it has nearly unique electrical properties. Since most of our future energy will be generated, transmitted, and consumed in the form of electricity, copper will always be in demand. Our model confirms this. However, similar arguments can be raised for other metals, such as lead, zinc, tin, tungsten, and silver. Each is particularly useful in providing certain services because of its own particular combination of properties. History provides strong support for the enduring importance of these metals, for there are no metals that have fallen into disuse. As time passes the number of metals in use grows, and with one or two exceptions, such as mercury, the demand for each increases. We have not made a complete analysis for any other scarce metal, but we strongly suspect that if we did a pattern of future use similar to that predicted for copper would emerge.

We might then ask whether the availability of copper resources is in any way unique. Again, the answer is no. Copper is one of the geochemically scarce metals—that is, one of those present in the earth's crust at concentrations below about 0.1 percent; any such metal that has essential industrial uses will eventually have to be produced from backstop resources. The moment when these must be tapped varies from metal to metal, depending on the extent of resources and the level of use, but historical and geochemical evidence suggests that the relative order in which the backstop resources will be utilized for the technologically important metals can be predicted from the average abundance of each metal in the earth's crust (Skinner 1976). Gold, silver, tin, lead, copper, and zinc are expected to be extracted from the backstop resources in that order. We believe the qualitative results we have obtained for copper will apply to these other metals as well.

Materials Scarcity in a Macroeconomic Perspective

We end with some speculations about how the exhaustion of low-cost mineral resources may hinder future economic growth. A rigorous answer to this question would require us to perform a materials-modeling exercise for about 15 elements and another 30 to 50 or so important compounds; it is likely that we would know the answer before that research could be completed. Instead we shall draw on the copper model and related studies to estimate the economic consequences of progressive exhaustion of scarce mineral resources. We emphasize that this discussion is not based on an analysis of the mining, recycling, and possibilities for substitution of these minerals, but on the assumption that the pattern of exhaustion of copper ores also describes qualitatively the future of the other scarce minerals.

In 1979 the value of the production of all nonfuel minerals and metals that are not superabundant was around $6 billion, compared with $3 billion for copper.[2] If the exhaustion patterns of these minerals are similar to those of copper, the drag on economic growth due to scarcity of all nonfuel, exhaustible mineral resources might be three times that which we have estimated for copper. Our estimate of the cost of the intrinsic economic scarcity of copper was about 0.5 percent of the total national output (NNP), both discounted over the next 180 years. For all the scarce nonfuel minerals, then, the discounted costs might be about 1.5 percent of NNP.

An alternative way of representing this cost would be to ask what fraction of future NNP must be devoted to meeting the demands for services now met by copper. In 1970 the cost of meeting copper services was about 0.12 percent of NNP. Our calculations show that this cost will rise to 1.2 percent of NNP by the year 2100. After that time new copper will be obtained from backstop resources and the share of copper and its substitutes in NNP will remain approximately constant. Thus NNP is reduced by 1.2 percent over this period by the increasing scarcity of copper. If we apply our factor of three for the other scarce minerals, we can estimate that in the year 2100 the scarcity of all nonfuel mineral resources will reduce NNP by 3.6 percent. The drag on economic growth due to the intrinsic scarcity of copper alone is 0.0095 percent per annum throughout this period; the drag due to the intrinsic scarcity of copper and all other scarce nonfuel minerals would be 0.029 per annum.[3] During this period the projected economic growth is 2.54 percent per annum; the total drag due to scarcity of all nonfuel minerals might, then, lower the rate of economic growth by about one hundredth.

Our estimated drag of 0.029 percent per annum may be an underestimate, the most important reason being the assumption that all the scarce metals can be replaced by abundant substitutes. Much of our experience with the use of substitutes for scarce materials involves the replacement of one scarce material by another that is more abundant but nevertheless geochemically scarce, as when molybdenum is used to replace tungsten as an alloying ingredient in steel. It remains to be demonstrated that all the geochemically scarce metals can be replaced by abundant ones. The fact that modern technology has tended to make increased use of scarce and exotic metals suggests that this demonstration may not be easy. Copper is not representative of the scarce metals used in many high-technology applications, which often depend directly on the properties of particular materials, as in the case of niobium, used to make superconducting alloys.

The second reason the estimated economic drag may be too low is that our model for copper assumes the supports required for processing the backstop resources will be available and the environmental consequences of their use will be accepted. But the scale of backstop enterprises is immense by today's standard. The projected rate of mining copper backstop resources would require the excavation and processing of about 13 cubic kilometers of rock a year in the United States. This would mean the simultaneous operation of 275 open-pit mines the size of the Bingham Canyon copper mine today, the use of a supply of fresh water equal to 20 percent of the discharge of the Mississippi River, and the generation of electric power equivalent to the entire power production of the world today for this purpose alone. Such operations might have to be multiplied three-fold to allow for the replacement of other geochemically scarce minerals by abundant ones (if that is technically possible). We do not say that these events are unlikely, and we must always be cautious about a linear projection of current data into the distant future. But the mere scale of the backstop mining industry gives us pause, and we should not underestimate the technological and political obstacles that lie in the way.

A New Iron Age?

We end our study where we began. The economy is incessantly engaged in a struggle between two forces, advances in technology that enhance the productivity of labor and the exhaustion of resources that diminish it. Over the last two centuries technology has been the clear victor. But what of the future? Our tentative view, seen in the faint light shed by the copper model, is that mineral exhaustion will indeed hinder economic growth but that the drag need not be large. This conclusion must be qualified, for it rests on two central assumptions. First, society must find acceptable ways to use its superabundant backstop resources of the geochemically scarce metals and minerals. Mining on a very large scale would have to be permitted and the availability of abundant energy and process water assured. The second condition is that technology must succeed in finding substitutes for the services provided by metals and minerals that now appear to have unique properties, such as the silver used in photography.

Are we poised to enter a New Iron Age? We think so. Over the next two centuries, as industrial economies continue to grow and as poor countries become affluent, the low-cost but limited resources of copper and other geochemically scarce minerals will be largely exhausted. The globe's economies will gradually come to depend upon superabundant resources such as iron, silica, and aluminum. But as the scarce minerals disappear, key industrial processes—transportation, communication, combustion—will not vanish. Rather they will be adapted to new conditions, most particularly to a reliance on the superabundant minerals.

Will the New Iron Age mark an economic decline or even a return to a subsistence economy? We think not. Even without major technological advances, existing resources should allow sufficient substitution, recycling, and use of high-cost ores to provide today's products, processes, and services in the future. Many of the services now performed by copper and other geochemically scarce minerals will be taken over by the geochemically abundant minerals. Other, absolutely vital services will be met with recycled and backstop mining of the scarce resources. As long as society does not severely hamper substitution, recycling, and backstop production, the passing of scarce minerals from the economic scene need not drag advanced nations down to a preindustrial standard of living.

But the difficulties of making the transition to the new era should not be underestimated. We may find it as painful to enter the New Iron Age as it was for our forebears to escape the original one.

Notes
References
Index

Notes

1. Introduction

1. The conditions sufficient for existence and optimality of a general economic equilibrium can be found in most advanced treatises or textbooks on microeconomics.

2. One of the earliest statements of the correspondence principle is in Samuelson (1966).

3. We now can see why the strange concept of present-value prices is so useful. Present-value prices allow all economic calculations to be put on an equivalent footing by translating transactions at different points of time into equivalent units. Put differently, since present-value prices are an accounting unit wherein all transactions occur at a given place at time zero, the economic value of events occurring at different points of time and space are economically equivalent. This equivalence is clearly not present for efficiency prices, which occur at different points of time and, because money has different values at different points of time, have different intrinsic economic values even though they might be in the same currency.

4. The notion of dual variables or shadow prices goes back to the dawn of linear-programming theory. Full expositions are provided in Dantzig (1963), chap. 6; Gale (1960), chap. 1; and Tucker (1957). The term applies generally to the value of an activity or a resource and should not be construed narrowly in terms of resource economics or the value of copper.

5. In technical terms, the variable w is the dual variable or shadow price associated with the resource-scarcity constraint in inequality (1.2). In this context the dual variable is the derivative of the objective function in (1.1) with respect to the parameter of the constraint in (1.2); this parameter is the total available quantity of copper (1,500 billion pounds), and the derivative has the dimension of dollars per pound. Other constraints have associated dual variables, and these will also have important economic interpretations. For example, each constraint in the demand equations in (1.3) will have an associated dual variable that can be interpreted as the price that consumers will pay for an additional unit of copper services.

6. We use the term "royalty" by analogy with the monetary payment to a landowner who allows others to remove minerals or fuels from a property. In competitive markets the royalty paid by a firm to a landowner for such rights, when such royalty is calculated per unit resource extracted, will be exactly the royalty as here defined.

3. Substitution, Recycling, and Demand

1. We will show later that this type of substitution is expected to be relatively unimportant for copper in the future.

2. Examples of services that can be obtained from only one metal are the use of mercury in the extraction of gold by amalgamation and the use of silver in the light-sensitive salts required in photography. In such cases substitution may be accomplished through the use of alternative processes rather than alternative materials— the cyanide process for gold extraction in place of amalgamation or the digital storage of the information required to reconstruct an image, for example.

3. For the early history of the use of copper and iron see Tylecote 1976.

4. A full account of the calculation of the substitution costs for all of the demand categories will be found in Gordon and Hummel (1982).

5. Allowance for the thermal resistance of the boundary layers would slightly reduce the size difference computed for the copper and aluminum radiators.

6. The creep rate of a metal under stress scales as T/T_m, where T is the temperature and T_m is the melting temperature of the metal in °K. Because the melting temperature of aluminum is lower than that of copper, creep is relatively greater in aluminum wire.

7. See Nordhaus, Gordon, and Hummel (1982) for a detailed explanation of the procedures used.

8. Unitary income elasticity implies that, if the relative prices of copper and other goods are unchanged, then demand for copper-equivalent services grows at the same rate as national income. Zero price elasticity signifies that there is no effect of a change in relative prices on the total demand for copper-equivalent services. Under these conditions, the demand for copper services takes the form $D =$ (constant) $\times$ (national income).

5. Findings of the Copper Model

1. As defined in Chapter 2, a technology or resource is a backstop resource if it is superabundant; a backstop resource is capable of meeting all demand at a constant real cost for an indefinitely long period.

2. Perhaps the most unsatisfactory single datum used in this study is the estimate of the cost of substitution for electronic wire. We estimate that aluminum will be the substitute, but that it will be much more costly because soldering cannot be used for aluminum joints. We were not able to make what we considered a reliable estimate of the incremental costs of using aluminum in this application because there is little industrial experience with this particular substitution. The effects of this variable on the model are examined later, in the section on sensitivity analysis (run 5C). We may think of the electronic wire category as a proxy for any use of copper for which it proves difficult to find a low-cost substitute.

3. We assume that only 80 percent of the copper scrap stock can be recycled, so the disappearance of the stocks of scrap implies the recycling of the full 80 percent.

4. An interesting historical parallel can be seen here. According to a private communication from personnel at Bell Labs, this kind of substitution has already occurred in telecommunications. If all telephonic communications took place through paired copper wires, as was the case in the 1880s and 1890s, rather than through microwave or multiplexed coaxial cable as today, the total amount of copper required would be 10 times today's copper requirements in communications. If the gauge of copper wire used today were as large as that 100 years ago, the requirement would be even higher.

5. Total deliveries are 3×10^9 kilograms times \$125 per kilogram = \$375 $\times$ 10^9, as compared with 1978 Net National Product of \$1,910 $\times$ 10^9.

6. The technical definition of these three indexes is the following. Let x_i = copper metal consumption, q_i = copper-equivalent service consumption, p_i = the price of copper-equivalent services, and t = time in years. Then

$$I_1(t) = \frac{\sum_i p_i(t)\, x_i(1975)}{\sum_i p_i(1975)\, x_i(1975)},$$

$$I_2(t) = \frac{\sum_i p_i(t)\, q_i(1975)}{\sum_i p_i(1975)\, q_i(1975)},$$

$$I_3(t) = \exp\left\{ \frac{\sum_i \log\left[\frac{p_i(t)}{p_i(1975)}\right] p_i(1975)\, q_i(1975)}{\sum_i p_i(1975)\, q_i(1975)} \right\}.$$

7. We are unaware of any previous work on balanced technological change for multisector models, although this proposition is well-known for one-sector models, where balanced technological change is referred to as "Harrod-neutral" or "labor-augmenting" technological change. The proof is as follows. Suppressing all time subscripts where inessential, let $\mathbf{x}$ = the vector of gross outputs for n goods, $\mathbf{y}$ = the vector of final demands, and $\mathbf{L}$ = the vector of m exogenously given, primary (or nonproduced) inputs. Good i is produced according to a constant-returns-to-scale production function, $\mathbf{x}_i = F^i(\mathbf{x}_{ji}, \mathbf{L}_i)$, where $\mathbf{x}_{ji}$ = the inputs of good j into the production of good i and $\mathbf{L}_i$ = the input vector of primary inputs into the production of good i. We can write this succinctly as $\mathbf{x} = F(\mathbf{x}, \mathbf{L})$.

At each point of time, let $\mathbf{b}$ and $\mathbf{b}_0$ be, respectively, ($n \times n$)- and ($n \times m$)-dimensional matrixes of unit inputs of produced and primary inputs that minimize costs of production. Further designate $\mathbf{p}$ = vector of prices of produced goods (that is, the prices of $\mathbf{x}$) and $\mathbf{w}$ = vector of prices of primary inputs (that is, the prices of the $\mathbf{L}$). Then the zero-profit condition implies that $\mathbf{p} = \mathbf{bp} + \mathbf{b}_0\mathbf{w}$, where the prices and input coefficients may vary over time as supplies and demands change. Under balanced technological change, we can rewrite the production function as $\mathbf{x} = F(\mathbf{x}, A_t\mathbf{L})$, where A_t is a function of time and t is a scalar representing the uniform level of balanced factor-augmenting technological change.

We can redefine $\mathbf{L}^* = A_t\mathbf{L}$ as the "efficiency units" of the primary inputs. Then the production function becomes stationary as $\mathbf{x} = F(\mathbf{x}, \mathbf{L}^*)$. Under balanced technological change, the efficiency inputs of primary inputs are $\mathbf{b}_{0t}^* = \mathbf{b}_{0t}/A_t$. If the input prices are uniquely determined, then the primary-input prices at each point of time under balanced technological change are given by $\mathbf{w}_t^* = \mathbf{w}_t A_t$. This implies that prices are given by $\mathbf{p}_t = \mathbf{bp}_t + \mathbf{b}_{0t}^* \mathbf{w}_t^* = \mathbf{bp}_t + (\mathbf{b}_{0t}/A_t)(\mathbf{w}_t A_t) = \mathbf{bp}_t + \mathbf{b}_{0t}\mathbf{w}_t$. This is the identical condition as the solution with no technological change, thereby demonstrating that balanced technological change has no effect on the relative prices of produced goods.

8. Many of the costs of market imperfections are surveyed in E. Denison (1962). More recent estimates are contained in F. M. Scherer (1980).

9. This calculation is one in which the assumption of inelastic demand for copper-equivalent services is particularly inapt. With the large price rises in some services, it seems likely that the bundle of consumer goods actually consumed may tilt away from copper-intensive ones.

10. Some of the cases cannot be compared because of technical reasons, such as different discount rates.

6. Toward a New Iron Age

1. An efficient pattern of exhaustion is a pattern of resource use that minimizes the cost of providing the services obtained from the resource and its substitutes throughout the time period covered by the model.

2. Resources in limited supply include asbestos, boron, fluorspar, helium, mica, phosphate, potash, soda, sulfur, antimony, lead, manganese, mercury, molybdenum, nickel, silver, tungsten, vanadium, and zinc.

3. Drag is calculated as the difference in economic growth between (1) the case where real copper prices remain constant and (2) the base case. Thus, where the drag is due to copper alone, NNP growth slows from 2.54 percent per annum to 2.5307 percent per annum.

References

Agterberg, F. P. 1980. Geochemical abundance models. *AIME Transactions* 268:1823–1830.

Agterberg, F. P., and S. R. Divi. 1978. A statistical model for the distribution of copper, lead, and zinc in the Canadian Appalachian region. *Economic Geology* 73:230–245.

Ahrens, L. H. 1954. The lognormal distribution of the elements—a fundamental law of geochemistry and its subsidiary. *Geochimica et Cosmochimica Acta* 5:49–73, 6:121–131.

Arthur D. Little, Inc. 1978. *Economic impact of environmental regulations on the U.S. copper industry.* Cambridge, Mass.: Arthur D. Little, Inc.

Barnett, Harold J., and C. Morse. 1963. *Scarcity and growth: The economics of resource availability.* Baltimore: Johns Hopkins University Press.

Bever, Michael B. 1976. The recycling of metals—II. Nonferrous metals. *Conservation and Recycling* 1:137–147.

Biswas, A. K., and W. G. Davenport, 1980. *Extractive metallurgy of copper,* 2nd ed. Oxford: Pergamon Press.

Brink, J. W. 1971. The prediction of mineral resources and long-term price trends in the non-ferrous metal mining industry is no longer Utopian. *Errospectra* 10:46–56.

Brobst, D. A., and W. P. Pratt, eds. 1973. *United States mineral resources.* U.S. Geological Survey Professional Paper 820. Washington, D.C.

Brown, Harrison S. 1954. *The challenge of man's future.* New York: Viking Press.

Brown, J. M., and B. C. Field. 1979. *Possibilities for natural resource substitution in the U.S. economy.* National Science Foundation Report NSF/RA 790250. Washington, D.C.

Carrillo, F. V., M. H. Hibpsham, and R. D. Rosenkranz. 1974. *Recovery of secondary copper and zinc in the United States.* U.S. Bureau of Mines Information Circular 8622. Washington, D.C.

Chapman, P. F., and F. Roberts. 1983. *Metal resources and energy.* London: Butterworths.

Charles River Associates, Inc. 1970. *Economic analysis of the copper industry.* Cambridge, Mass.: Charles River Associates.

——— 1978. *The economics and geology of Mineral supply: An integrated framework for long-run policy analysis.* Cambridge, Mass.: Charles River Associates.

Clark, A. L. 1971. Strata-bound copper sulfides in the Precambrian Belt Super-group, northern Idaho and northwestern Montana. *Society of Mining Geologists of Japan,* special issue 3, pp. 261–267.

COMRATE [Committee on Mineral Resources and the Environment, National Research Council]. 1975. Resources of copper. In *Mineral resources and the environment,* chap. 5. Washington, D.C.: National Academy of Sciences.

Cooper, Richard N. 1975. Resource needs revisited. *Brookings Papers on Economic Activity* I:238–245.

Copper Development Association. 1957. *Copper through the ages.* London: Copper Development Association.

Cox, D. P. 1979. The distribution of copper in common rocks and ore deposits. In *Copper in the environment,* part 1, ed., J. O. Nriagu. New York: Wiley.

Cox, D. P., and others. 1973. Copper. In *United States mineral resources,* ed. D. A. Brobst and W. P. Pratt. U.S. Geological Survey Professional Paper 820, pp. 163–189. Washington, D.C.

Dantzig, George B. 1963. *Linear Programming and Extensions.* Princeton, N.J.: Princeton University Press.

Deffeyes, K., and I. MacGregor. 1978. *Uranium distribution in mined deposits and in the earth's crust.* Report for the U.S. Department of Energy, prepared under Bendix Field Engineering Corporation, Grand Junction Operations, subcontract 76-002-L, and Bendix contract EY-76-1664. Grand Junction, Colo.: U.S. Department of Energy.

Denison, Edward F. 1962. *The sources of economic growth in the United States and the alternatives before us.* New York: Committee for Economic Development.

Erickson, R. L. 1973. *Crustal abundance of elements, and mineral reserves and resources.* U.S. Geological Survey Professional Paper 820, pp. 21–25. Washington, D.C.

Fisher, F. M., P. H. Cootner, and M. N. Baily. 1972. An econometric model of the world copper industry. *Bell Journal of Economics* 3:568–609.

Fisher, J. C., and R. H. Pry. 1971. A simple substitution model of technological change. *Technological Forecasting and Social Change* 3:75–88.

Franklin Institute. 1974. *National controlled study of relative risk of overheating of aluminum compared with copper wired receptacles in homes and laboratory.* Franklin Research Center Report F-C 4812-01. Philadelphia.

Gale, David. 1960. *Theory of Linear Economic Models.* New York: McGraw.

Gluschke, W., J. Shaw, and B. Varon. 1979. *Copper: The next fifty years.* Dordrecht, Holland: D. Reidel.

Goeller, H. E., and A. M. Weinberg. 1976. The age of substitutability. *Science* 191:683–689.

Goldich, S. S., and others. 1966. Geochronology of the midcontinent region, United States. I. Scope, methods and principles. *Journal of Geophysical Research* 71:5375–5388.

Gordon, R. B. 1982. Cost of substitution for scarce resources. In *Analytical techniques for studying substitution among materials,* ed. U.S. National Materials Advisory Board. Publication NMAB-385. Washington, D.C.: National Academy Press.

Gordon, R. B., and H. H. Hummel. 1982. Cost of substitution for copper. Materials Modeling Project Working Paper No. 4, Yale University, New Haven, Conn.

Harris, C. C. 1966. On the role of energy in comminution. *Transactions of the Institute of Mining and Metallurgy* C75:37–56.

Harrison, J. E. 1972. Precambrian Belt basin of northwestern United States: Its geometry, sedimentation, and copper occurences. *Geological Society of America Bulletin* 83:1215–1240.

Hartley, J. N., K. A. Prisbrey, and O. J. Wick. 1978. Chemical additives for ore grinding: How effective are they? *Engineering and Mining Journal* 179, no. 10:105–111.

Herfindahl, Orris C. 1959. *Copper costs and prices, 1870–1957.* Baltimore: Johns Hopkins Press.

Hibbard, Walter R., Jr., and others. 1977. A long-range model of the copper industry in the United States. Virginia Polytechnic Institute, Blacksburg, Virginia. Unpublished.

Hubbert, M. K. 1969. Energy resources. In *Resources and man,* ed. National Research Council, pp. 157–242. San Francisco. W. H. Freeman.

INCO [International Nickel Company]. 1975. Description of operating concepts required to establish preoperational monitoring of INCO's proposed Spruce Road project. Toronto, Ontario, Canada. Unpublished.

Jevons, William S. 1866. *The coal question.* London.

Joe, E. G. 1979. Energy consumption in Canadian mills. *Canadian Mining and Metallurgical Bulletin* 72, no. 806:147–151.

Kellogg, H. H. 1977. Sizing up the energy requirements for producing primary materials. *Engineering and Mining Journal* 178:61–65.

Kendrick, John W. 1961. *Productivity trends in the United States.* Princeton: Princeton University Press.

King, P. B. 1969. Tectonic map of North America. Washington, D.C.: U.S. Geological Survey.

Koopmans, Tjalling C. 1973. Some observations on optimal economic growth and exhaustible resources. In *Economic structure and development: Essays in honor of Jan Tinbergen,* ed. H. C. Bos, H. Linnemann, and P. de Wolff. New York: American Elsevier.

Lind, Robert C. 1982. *Discounting for time and risk in energy policy.* Washington, D.C.: Resources for the Future; dist., Baltimore: The Johns Hopkins University Press.

Lovering, T. S. 1969. Mineral resources from the land. In *Resources and man,* ed. National Research Council. San Francisco: W. H. Freeman.

Lyneis, J. E. 1982. Modeling the dynamics of substitution. In *Analytical techniques for studying substitution among materials,* ed. U.S. National Materials Advisory Board. Publication NMAB-385. Washington, D.C.: National Academy Press.

McKelvey, V. E. 1960. Relation of the reserves of the elements to their crustal abundances. *American Journal of Science* 258A:234–241.

Mathur, S. C., and J. P. Clark. 1983. An econometric analysis of substitution between copper and aluminum in the electrical conductor industry. *Materials and Society* 7:115–124.

Meadows, H. D., and others. 1970. The *Limits to growth: A report for the Club of Rome's project on the predicament of mankind.* New York: New American Library.

Mikesell, Raymond F. 1979. *The world copper industry: Structure and economic analysis.* Baltimore: Johns Hopkins University Press for Resources for the Future.

Mittleman, Joseph. 1969. Connecting aluminum wire reliability. *Electronics,* Dec. 8, p. 94.

National Bureau of Standards. 1974. *NBS Quarterly Report on Aluminum Wiring,* April 1974, p. E-17.

NATO [North Atlantic Treaty Organization]. 1976. *Rational use of potentially scarce materials.* Brussels: NATO Scientific Affairs Division.

Newman, Rae. 1975. *Hazard analysis of aluminum wiring.* U.S. Product Safety Commission, Report N11C-0600-25-H006.

Nordhaus, William D. 1973. The allocation of energy resources. *Brookings Papers on Economic Activity* 3:529–576.

────── 1979. *The efficient use of energy resources.* New Haven, Conn.: Yale University Press.

Nordhaus, W. D., R. B. Gordon, and H. H. Hummel. 1982. Materials modeling in copper: Demand. Materials Modeling Working Paper No. 5, Yale University, New Haven, Conn.

Nordhaus, W. D., and J. Tobin. 1972. Is growth obsolete? In *Economic growth.* New York: National Bureau of Economic Research; dist., New York: Columbia University Press

Nordhaus, W. D., and G. Yohe. 1983. Future paths of energy and carbon dioxide emissions. In *Changing climate: Report of the Carbon Dioxide Assessment Committee.* Washington, D.C.: National Academy Press.

O'Hara, T. A. 1980. Quick guides to the evaluation of orebodies. *CIM Bulletin* 73, no. 814:87–99.

Olby, R. 1982. Britain's resources of coal and spent uranium fuel. *Nature* 296:797–801.

Olson, Sherry H. 1971. *The depletion myth: A history of railroad use of timber.* Cambridge, Mass.: Harvard University Press.

Paley commission [U.S. President's Materials Policy Commission]. 1952. *Resources for freedom.* Washington, D.C.

Pearce, D. W., and J. Rose, eds. 1975. *The economics of natural resource depletion*. New York: John Wiley and Sons.

Peck, L., R. C. Nolen-Hoeksema, C. C. Barton, and R. B Gordon. 1985. Measurement of the resistance of imperfectly elastic rock to the propagation of tensile cracks. *Journal of Geophysical Research* 90:7827–7836.

Peterson, U., and R. S. Maxwell. 1983. Historical mineral production and price trends. *Mining Engineering,* January, pp. 24–34.

Pimenthal, D., and others. 1973. Food production and the energy crisis. *Science* 182:443–449.

Queneau, P. E. 1981. Coppermaking in the eighties—productivity in metal extraction from sulfide concentrates. *Journal of Metals* 33, no. 2:36–46.

Rosenberg, Nathan. 1973. Innovative responses to materials shortages. *American Economic Review* 43:111–118.

Samuelson, Paul A. 1966. Market mechanisms and maximization. In *The collected scientific papers of Paul A. Samuelson.* Cambridge, Mass.: MIT Press.

Scherer, F. M. 1980. *Industrial market structure and economic performance.* Chicago: Rand McNally.

Singer, D. A. 1977. Long-term adequacy of metal resources. *Resources Policy* 3:127–133.

Singer, D. A., and others. 1975. *Grade and tonnage relationships among copper deposits.* U.S. Geological Survey Professional Paper 907-E. Washington, D.C.

Skinner, B. J. 1976. A second Iron Age ahead? *American Scientist* 64:258–269.

——— 1979a. Earth resources. *Proceedings of the National Academy of Sciences* 76:4212–4217.

——— 1979b. The frequency of mineral deposits. *Geological Society of South Africa,* annex to vol. 82.

Slade, M. E. 1980a. An econometric model of the U.S. secondary copper industry: Recycling *vs.* disposal. *Journal of Environmental Economics and Management* 7:123–141.

——— 1980b. Price changes and metals markets: Modeling short- and long-run copper-aluminum substitution using Bayesian smoothness parameters. *Materials and Society* 4:1.

Smith, V. Kerry, ed. 1979. *Scarcity and growth reconsidered.* Baltimore: Johns Hopkins University Press for Resources for the Future.

Tilton, John E. 1977. *The future of nonfuel minerals.* Washington, D.C.: The Brookings Institution.

——— 1980. *Materials substitution: The experience of the tin-using industries.* College of Earth and Mineral Sciences, Pennsylvania State University, University Park. Unpublished.

Trinder, Barrie. 1982. *The making of the industrial landscape.* London: J. M. Dent & Sons.

Tucker, A. W. 1957. Linear and nonlinear programming. *Operations Research* 5:244–257.

Tylecote, Ronald F. 1976. *A history of metallurgy.* London: The Metals Society.

U.S. National Materials Advisory Board. 1982. *Analytical techniques for studying substitution among materials.* Publication NMAB-385. Washington, D.C.: National Academy Press.

Vogeley, W. A., ed. 1975. *Mineral materials modeling, A state-of-the-art review.* Baltimore: Johns Hopkins University Press for Resources for the Future.

Wills, B. A. 1981. *Mineral processing technology.* 2nd ed. Oxford: Pergamon Press.

Index